The NONPROFIT BUSINESS PLAN

The NONPROFIT BUSINESS PLAN

The Leader's Guide to Creating a Successful Business Model

David La Piana

Heather Gowdy

Lester Olmstead-Rose

Brent Copen

TURNER
PUBLISHING COMPANY

Turner Publishing Company

200 4th Avenue North • Suite 950 Nashville, Tennessee 37219
445 Park Avenue • 9th Floor New York, New York 10022

www.turnerpublishing.com

The Nonprofit Business Plan:
The Leader's Guide to Creating a Successful Business Model

Cover design by Mark Bergeron/Publishers' Design and Production
Services, Inc. and Gina Binkley
Book design by Glen Edelstein
Book artwork by Mark Bergeron/Publishers' Design and Production Services, Inc.

Library of Congress Cataloging-in-Publication Data
    The nonprofit business plan : the leader's guide to creating a
    successful business model / David La Piana ... [et al.].
       p. cm.
ISBN 978-1-61858-006-1
    1. Nonprofit organizations--Management. 2. Business planning.
I. La Piana, David, 1954-
HD62.6.N6543 2012
658.4'01--dc23
    2012025450

Printed in the United States of America
12 13 14 15 16 17 18—0 9 8 7 6 5 4 3 2 1

TABLE OF CONTENTS

ACKNOWLEDGMENTS

Special recognition goes to the team responsible for harnessing all of this thinking and putting it into a cohesive form. Heather Gowdy, Senior Manager for Research and Innovation, captained our team, bringing a deep knowledge of business planning and nonprofit consulting as well as a special skill for corralling her busy teammates. Lester Olmstead-Rose, a Partner who is our most senior strategic planner, was central to the team's effort, as was Brent Copen, a former colleague who is now a nonprofit CFO but remains an ongoing collaborator. The thinking represented in this book is a team effort, as was the writing.

PREFACE

Several years ago, my colleagues and I wrote *The Nonprofit Strategy Revolution*, creating a methodology that pushed beyond the limitations of traditional strategic planning. That approach—Real-Time Strategic Planning (RTSP)—was embraced by nonprofits seeking ways to align mission and vision with programmatic choices and operations within the context of an ever-changing external environment. But even as the *Revolution* was under way, our clients, grantmakers, and others in the sector began raising a common challenge: how can an organization obtain a sufficient grasp of the economic and operational implications of its strategic decisions and, in doing so, lay the groundwork for successful execution, execution that will truly accelerate growth and success? The difficulty stems partly from a lack of data, but, more important, the sector lacks a rigorous methodology for connecting mission to strategy to execution in a sustainable way.

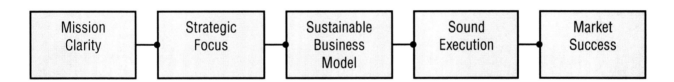

Absent a widely available methodology for making these connections, the nonprofit leaders with whom our firm is privileged to work were increasingly asking us to help them develop a "business plan" rather than a "strategic plan," although very often these terms had no precise definition. Working together with these clients to clarify and meet their needs, we have developed a methodology that roots strategic decision making in strong economic analysis, a methodology we call *DARE² Succeed*. The lessons and tools that form the core of that methodology are presented in this book.

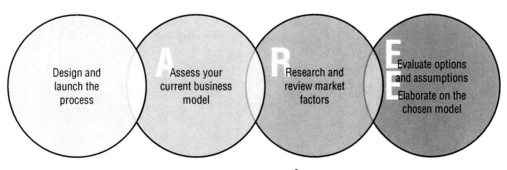

Business Planning: DARE² Succeed

As with all innovation projects at La Piana Consulting, this one is a team effort. Our consultants initiated the internal conversations leading to this book, first sharing what they were hearing from our clients and generating ideas regarding ways we might address these challenges. They continued to play a crucial role throughout the process as we tested emerging tools with clients and repeatedly squared our thinking with our experience in the field to make sure that the ideas you encounter in these pages represent practical and workable approaches to accelerating your organization's success.

The Nonprofit Business Plan is aimed at nonprofit leaders who want a deeper understanding of the choices, and consequences, they face in either continuing to pursue their current business model or changing it. Our audience includes nonprofit CEOs and other senior staff leaders, as well as staff members who aspire to future leadership roles. It also includes board members who seek a deeper understanding of their organization's business model and those who come from the corporate world and have been told that "the nonprofit sector is different." Indeed it is, and we hope this book will help these readers to see how to apply their commercial experience in the social sector. This book will also be of interest to foundation program officers seeking a better understanding of the organizational health of their grantees or an assessment of the likelihood of success of a new venture for which a grant seeker has requested support. It will be of help to our fellow consultants, who are increasingly asked to help nonprofits create business plans and, in so doing, support fundamental organizational transformation. Finally, this book may be of interest to students enrolled in graduate-level nonprofit management programs and their instructors. Collectively, this audience constitutes our colleagues. To them, we offer our own learning as a spur to conversation and continued learning for us all.

David La Piana
June 2012

HOW THIS BOOK IS ORGANIZED

The Nonprofit Business Plan proceeds from the more general to the more specific. In this way, a general-interest reader who does not intend to actually produce a business plan—at least not now—can begin at the beginning and continue reading until the level of specificity moves beyond what he or she is looking for. Meanwhile, the reader for whom this book is a guide to creating an actual business plan can also begin at the beginning and just keep going.

Chapter 1 begins by defining business planning, then compares and contrasts business planning with strategic planning, and provides guidance on determining when each might be needed.

Chapter 2 introduces the concept of a planning team and presents six questions that every planning team should answer at the beginning of the business planning process.

Chapter 3 focuses on the nonprofit business model, and provides a method for assessing the health of an organization's current business model as a way to understand and—if necessary—change it.

Chapter 4 addresses market research, identifying the basic questions that need to be answered before launching any new program, partnership, entity, or growth strategy, and suggesting methods for finding answers to those questions.

Chapter 5 presents our basic framework for creating a business plan, identifying the key questions that a business plan must answer, and describing some additional ways organizations can go about finding answers to those questions. It also provides a model table of contents for a business plan.

Chapter 6 focuses on the economic and financial aspects of a business plan, providing both a broad overview and specific tools nonprofit leaders can use. It is intended for the generalist and the manager rather than the financial specialist. It requires understanding your numbers and points out where you should engage your CFO, accountant, or Board Treasurer to provide deeper analysis.

Chapter 7 walks through the sections of a typical business plan and reviews what should be included in each.

Chapter 8 answers the question: now that I have all this information, what do I do with it? It presents a way of approaching decision making that will engage key constituencies from funders to staff. It also addresses the difficult situation in which your effort produces a business plan that proves conclusively that your exciting new idea won't work.

Finally, an **Appendix** offers a sample business plan.

The NONPROFIT BUSINESS PLAN

CHAPTER 1

WHAT IS A NONPROFIT BUSINESS PLAN AND WHY DO YOU NEED ONE?

Consider the following statements:

> *"Business planning is for businesses, and strategic planning is for nonprofits."*

> *"A business plan is just a strategic plan with numbers attached."*

> *"I don't need a business plan, I need a business case."*

These are some of the statements we have heard from clients in the course of discussing and engaging in business planning over the last several years. Each is built on certain assumptions common in the nonprofit sector.

> *"Business planning is for businesses, and strategic planning is for nonprofits."*

This statement revives the old concept of nonprofit exceptionalism. After being told for more than two decades that they should operate more like businesses, nonprofits sometimes rebel, asserting that the distinct role, financing, and culture of most nonprofits make them completely different from businesses. We prefer Paul Light's now-classic exhortation that, in response to such arguments, nonprofits should try to become "more nonprofit-like."[1] That is, nonprofits live in an economic world just as businesses do, but they have an essentially different function in society and therefore need to use caution in adopting business tools and business thinking wholesale. The bottom line: a nonprofit needs a business plan just as much as a business does, perhaps more so given the narrower room for experimentation and the high consequences of failure—both of which can be traced back to often narrow operating mar-

---

1. Light, Paul C. "Nonprofit-like: Tongue Twister or Aspiration?" *The Nonprofit Quarterly*, Vol 8, Issue 2 (2001)

gins and lack of adequate capital. But that business plan must be tailored to the unique needs of each nonprofit as it navigates its own complex path. Just as a manufacturing-company executive would not tolerate being forced into a business planning process designed for a retail business, nonprofits need a business planning process that fits with their sector's and their organization's requirements.

"A business plan is just a strategic plan with numbers attached."

This second statement implies that a strategic plan is still the basic document required for establishing a nonprofit's direction and that to undertake business planning simply means adding a budget to that document, perhaps in an appendix. Such an approach reflects a missed opportunity. A solid business plan goes beyond articulation of strategy and projection of revenues and expenses: it delves into the organization's economic logic and operational requirements, testing leadership's assumptions and showing how and why the budget presented is likely to be sustainable in the long term. It informs strategy, rather than being purely derivative of it.

"I don't need a business plan, I need a business case."

This statement reflects both a bit of discomfort with the idea of business planning and a common concern among those seeking to create one. Often, nonprofits desire first and foremost a "case statement" for fundraising, a document that will persuade investors to fund the proposed venture. Once they enter the business planning process, however, even the most reluctant nonprofit leaders usually become enthusiastically engaged in understanding at a deeper level the enterprise or activity for which they seek to raise funds. Of course, a solid business plan is indeed a great fundraising tool, but that is a secondary benefit; the primary value comes from engagement in a rigorous, analytical process that drives strategic, mission-oriented decisions.

CASE STUDY

An animal services agency wants to end its government contract for animal control so that it can become a no-kill shelter—a major programmatic shift. The board votes to move forward based on the mission imperative and a review of some basic financial data related to the savings that would accrue from eliminating the animal-control positions; it anticipates attracting new funding to cover other program costs. One year after severing the contract, the organization finds itself in financial crisis and is forced to dramatically reduce its public-education, animal-adoption, and shelter programs because donors didn't step up as hoped.

What went wrong? In large part, the organization's crisis could be traced to the absence of a thorough analysis of the shared costs that had been covered by the government contract, an honest assessment of the likelihood that new donors would come forward in light of the programmatic shift, and a plan for ensuring sustainability until that happened.

BUSINESS PLANNING DEFINED

Nonprofits often use the terms *strategic planning* and *business planning* interchangeably, but a good business plan goes beyond the traditional strategic plan with its focus on mission and vision, goals, and objectives. A business plan tests the proposition that a particular undertaking—program, partnership, new venture, growth strategy, or the entity as a whole—is economically and operationally viable. It provides a window into the drivers of economic success (including market factors) and the scale, structure, leadership, staffing, timeline, costs, and risks that must be examined and negotiated for the venture to succeed.

DEFINITION

A business plan tests the proposition that a particular undertaking—program, partnership, new venture, growth strategy, or the entity as a whole—is economically and operationally viable.

Although much has been written about business planning in the corporate sector, it is not sufficient to take the basic pieces of corporate business planning and simply insert the word *nonprofit* in each. Nonprofits live in a different economic world from that inhabited by corporations. They have different priorities and aims and derive their funding in different ways. The nonprofit business planning process must integrate these uniquely nonprofit elements with the unavoidable reality of any economic enterprise; it must generate enough cash to cover its expenses, both capital and operating, or it will fail, no matter how noble or essential the mission.

WHAT MAKES NONPROFITS DIFFERENT

MARKET FAILURE. One of the defining features of the nonprofit sector is its focus on the provision of goods or services that are not profitable (or profitable enough) to incent businesses to provide them in sufficient quantities. Nonprofits must make up the market shortfall by attracting other sources of revenue, including third-party payers.

THIRD-PARTY PAYERS. A nonprofit organization's "customers" are not just the individuals and groups availing themselves of a particular product or service. Given that those customers typically do not pay market rate for what they receive, the nonprofit must make up the difference with funding from other sources, including individual donors, foundations, and government. Those third-party payers are also customers, although they may not receive anything directly in return. Nonprofits must continually consider, attract, and satisfy both types of customer. Remember, too, that third-party funding is essential to most nonprofit activities, not just those aimed at helping the poor. A seat at the opera or admission to an art exhibit is just as likely to be subsidized by donors as is a soup kitchen or youth-mentoring program.

PRIMACY OF THE MISSION. While the "double (even triple) bottom line"[2] is getting more attention in all sectors, nonprofits are legally bound to prioritize mission advancement over profit maximization. The choices they make as a result of mission priorities may be different from those of a similarly focused for-profit; the consequences of those choices often put additional financial pressure on the nonprofit organization.

DIFFICULTY ACCESSING GROWTH CAPITAL. Venture capital, long a fixture of the for-profit sector, has only recently become a viable option for some nonprofits. There are still far too few funders (both individual and institutional) willing to invest large sums of money in nonprofits with growth plans, however.

THE VALUE OF A BUSINESS PLAN

Nonprofits regularly make crucial decisions, such as whether to undertake a capital campaign, open or expand a program, merge with another entity, buy or rent new office space, or change the pricing of a service offering. Even decisions as routine as hiring for a new position or giving staff a cost-of-living raise have long-term, far-reaching consequences.

---

2. References to the double bottom line typically refer to evaluating performance in both financial terms and with respect to positive social impact. A triple bottom line adds ecological, or environmental, impact.

To take one example common to every business, a 3% across-the-board pay raise today becomes part of tomorrow's base salary when next year another raise is considered. Thus, the impact of that 3% is far larger than it appears, when viewed over the long term. If an organization with $500,000 in salaries offers a modest 3% raise every year for ten years, at the end of that period, salary costs will increase by nearly $172,000, or about a third. Even in the short term, a 3% raise may increase payroll taxes, retirement contributions, and worker-compensation costs. This is not said to *discourage* giving raises or providing retirement benefits but rather to *encourage* taking stock of and planning for the consequences that will accrue tomorrow from today's decisions.

Financial decisions large and small ultimately increase or decrease stress on a nonprofit's business model: the interplay of an organization's scope (geographic, programmatic, and customer) with its economic logic (how it structures and pays for itself).[3] Business planning is a process through which decision makers can understand and anticipate these consequences. A business plan may be used to:

- Help a nonprofit recognize that its current business model is suboptimal or even outright broken.
- Test the proposition that growth will fix financial problems, especially in this era when "scaling up" is the holy grail of nonprofit financial strategy.
- Surface assumptions that may be overly rosy, identify negative trends, or expose wishful thinking that could lead to disaster if ignored.
- Evaluate and prepare for a significant change in scope—geographic, programmatic, or customer.

DEFINITION – NONPROFIT BUSINESS MODEL

The nonprofit business model is the interplay of an organization's scope (geographic, programmatic, and customer) with its economic logic (how it structures and pays for itself).

A good business plan describes the business model in such a way that those who read it—board members, donors, political leaders, and interested funders—are reassured that the proposed program, venture, partnership, or growth strategy really does "make sense" and has a high likelihood of success. Bold ideas supported by sound economic reasoning and a solid management team are more likely to garner support than equally great ideas accompanied by a general "just trust me" attitude. To accelerate your organization's work, you need sound, evidence-based decision making. Business plans are rapidly replacing strategic plans in this function as donors

---

3. La Piana, David. *Nonprofit Strategy Revolution: Real-Time Strategic Planning in a Rapid-Response World*. Saint Paul: Fieldstone Alliance, 2008

increasingly see themselves as investors and are paying far greater attention to the economic sustainability of the causes they support. They want to understand not just the idea but also how the idea makes economic sense, is sustainable, and can be brought to an appropriate scale.

BUSINESS PLANNING AND STRATEGIC PLANNING: THE ESSENTIAL DIFFERENCES

Ten years ago, one rarely heard of a nonprofit business plan. Strategic planning was all the rage. Like business plans, traditional strategic plans are filled with numbers: the number of individuals to be served, the dollars to be raised, the percentage change sought in the diversity of the board or staff, etc. But they are often weak on describing how these goals fit within a viable business model. Over time, as frustration with traditional strategic planning grew and as nonprofit board members and other supporters—particularly those from the corporate sector—increasingly asked for better data and analysis, nonprofits began to ask for business plans.

In our experience, however, what these nonprofits often wanted was still a traditional strategic plan, albeit one with a detailed budget included. To understand the difference between a strategic plan and a business plan, it helps to first differentiate between *strategy* and *planning*. We define strategy as *a coordinated set of actions aimed at creating and sustaining a competitive advantage in carrying out the mission.*[4] Planning brings strategy to life, adding the detail needed for implementation. As we discuss in depth in *The Nonprofit Strategy Revolution*, nonprofit leaders often rush into the "planning" phase of strategic planning, thus shortchanging themselves on the strategy front. Taking time at the outset to consider the organization's identity and business model, its market—including competitors, collaborators, and market trends—and the criteria it will use to make decisions in the face of emerging opportunities and challenges will pay dividends once the strategy-development process is over and "real life" necessitates adjustments to the implementation plan.

Nonprofits *need* sound strategies: organizational, programmatic, and operational.[5] They also need implementation plans. Successful strategic-planning processes typically yield the former, and many times include both. Often—though not always—organizations need to spend additional time examining and evaluating the economic and operational model that supports or will

---

4. Ibid.

5. *Organizational strategy* is the means a nonprofit uses to determine how it will advance its mission, realize its vision, and deliver real value to the community or cause it serves through successfully navigating competitive, collaborative, and other market dynamics. *Programmatic strategies* are the approaches, programs, and activities undertaken in order to achieve specific outcomes. Operational strategies are aimed at enhancing nonprofit's administrative efficiency, preparedness, and execution. They typically involve areas such as finance, human resources, communication, information technology, and governance.

support their program, venture, partnership, or growth strategy. It is at these times that a nonprofit should consider a business planning process. A small regional land trust, for example, may conclude through a strategic planning process that it needs to take a more networked approach to its work and purchase increasing amounts of land in partnership with others (organizational strategies); launch an initiative to support grassroots organizing in support of regional conservation issues (a programmatic strategy); and put in place both new technologies and a new model for volunteer training to facilitate online engagement among its grassroots supporters (operational strategies). An implementation plan is then created and serves as a roadmap for moving forward with each strategy. More than likely, a business plan will be needed to determine how the business model must adapt in pursuit of the new strategies. What will it cost to make these changes? If the land trust has historically depended on donations from individual landowners, will they support this change financially? Will new government funds be needed to acquire, protect, and manage increasing amounts of land? What are the assumptions and options around funding available through different sources? This land trust will have to look more deeply at the economic and operational implications of the strategic shift and create a business plan showing how the expansion will happen. The financial and operational planning will need to be more comprehensive than is typical in strategic planning and the risks and assumptions fully understood.

As this example demonstrates, an organization must have identified a strategy before it can productively engage in business planning. The strategy may be provisional—*we will proceed with this undertaking only if the business planning process proves that it is an economically and operationally viable way to advance our mission*—but board and staff must believe it promising enough to warrant investing time and money in a business planning process. Early in the process, the business plan informs the strategic decision; ultimately, it becomes central to successful implementation.

Strategies can come either from a traditional strategic planning process or, as shown in Figure A, from a more targeted strategy-formation process, part of what we call Real-Time Strategic Planning. An organization may find itself faced with a strategic opportunity, competitive challenge, or business model challenge at any time. For example, a theater may identify a new competitor—a performing arts center—that is planning to open in the near future and is attracting a lot of attention and resources for its planned shows, potentially leaving the theater with empty seats. This competitive challenge requires a response, and that response is likely to be in the form of a strategy. Perhaps the theater decides to approach the performing arts center and suggest a partnership focused on coordinated programming and joint marketing. Or perhaps it decides to cut ticket prices and add a greater variety of shows.

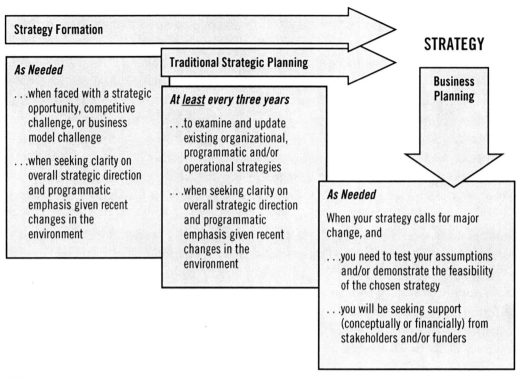

Figure A

Either response fits our definition of a strategy, stated earlier: *a coordinated set of actions designed to create and sustain a competitive advantage in achieving a nonprofit's mission.* Is the chosen path the right strategy for the theater? The board and management may be happy with the concept, and it may work to strengthen the theater's position as a fixture in the community. There will undoubtedly be economic considerations, however. What expenses will the theater incur as it launches and implements this strategy? Long term and without subsidy, will it be able to restore its previous level of ticket sales? What overlap exists between the two organizations' subscribers and donors, and how is either the partnership or the pricing strategy likely to affect contributions? Will the chosen strategy attract new audiences to the theaters' shows or just provide more options for the existing audience? If the answers to these questions are obvious, then the theater can move forward with negotiating the details of the partnership (assuming the performing arts center is on board) or advertising the ticket-price reduction. However, if the theater has weak financials, and if it is not sure how its constituents will respond or what is happening in the broader market around support for live performance (perhaps the community's overall theater attendance is in decline), it may need to take a closer look at its proposed strategy as an economic proposition. Through business planning, the theater (perhaps in cooperation with the performing arts center) could examine its market, operations, revenue and expense trends, and any anticipated capital investments (such as a new ticketing system that will allow the two theaters to integrate sales). It can test the strategy it has developed to see if it makes economic and operational sense.

To further distinguish between a strategic plan and a business plan, we need to distinguish between the *process* and the resulting *product*. Strategic planning is, at its best, the process of considering and making strategic decisions. Business planning is the process of determining the parameters of an economically and operationally successful undertaking. A strategic plan or business plan—the product—is simply the results of those respective processes consolidated into a written document. Take care to keep the processes and the products separate in your mind and not rush toward producing a written plan at the expense of the process through which the decisions recorded in the document are made. The value of a business plan, in particular, is directly related to the rigor of the planning process.

> Strategic planning is, at its best, the process of considering and making strategic decisions. Business planning is the process of determining the parameters of an economically and operationally successful undertaking.

> The value of a business plan is directly related to the rigor of the planning process.

THE RIGHT PLAN FOR THE SITUATION

Successful nonprofits are *always* scanning their environment and considering the potential impact of both external and internal realities. Strategic planning and business planning are two approaches to evaluating and elaborating on particular responses. By now, it should be fairly clear how the goals of each differ. To summarize:

Strategic Planning	Business Planning
Develop organizational responses to opportunities and challenges	Test the economic logic and operational feasibility of a proposed response
Articulate a strategy	Test and elaborate on core elements of the strategy
Define a program model	Show how the program model will be economically and operationally viable
Confirm the need for a change to the business model	Describe how and why the new business model will succeed
Determine a means to increase mission impact	Test the assumptions that prove the change is feasible

Every nonprofit should engage in strategic planning, either episodically or (ideally) on an ongoing basis. But the "deeper dive" of business planning may or may not be appropriate at a given point for a particular nonprofit. Here are some of the factors to consider when deciding whether you need a business plan:

- Have you identified one or more strategies (organizational or programmatic) that will require—or result in—significant change to your existing business model?
- Are you considering the launch of a new program, partnership, or entity?
- Are you considering a growth strategy for your existing organization?
- Are you considering some other major change to your program mix, operations, or economic model?
- Do key decision makers (e.g., board members, executive staff) have sufficient information to make a go/no-go decision with respect to what is being proposed?
- Can you demonstrate to potential funders that your undertaking is both compelling and economically and operationally viable—and thus is worthy of their support?
- Does the leadership team have enough information to create a comprehensive implementation plan?

Figure B incorporates this list into a "decision tree" to help you further evaluate your need for a business plan.

With that grounding, and assuming you have decided that you need to develop a business plan, let us now turn to a consideration of how to approach business planning.

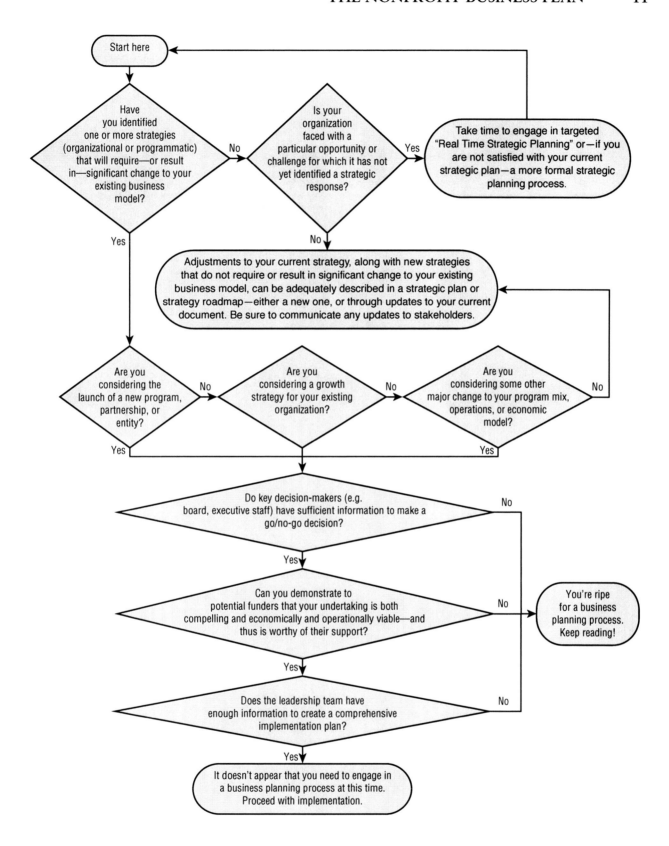

Figure B: Evaluating the Need for a Business Plan

CASE STUDY: ENERGY RETROFIT COLLABORATIVE

In one California county, a coalition of nonprofit, government, business, and labor groups came together with a vision: finding a way to finance energy retrofits for low-income households in their community. Environmental nonprofits liked the reduction in energy use the project would achieve, community groups were moved by the potential financial savings residents would realize, business saw an opportunity for more retrofit work, and labor saw that work as leading to more jobs and the opportunity to train workers for well-paying "green jobs." Local government, of course, liked all of it, so long as it didn't have to pay for it. Strategic planning led to an initiative where all these goals would be met. But several questions still remained. Would it work? What would it cost and how should it be structured? Through a robust business planning process, the working group articulated its assumptions about everything from timing to pricing to interest rates on the long-term capital that would fund the enterprise. By testing and adjusting those assumptions, the business planning exercise confirmed the economic viability of the initiative, defined the staffing and structure needed, exposed financial gaps that would have to be addressed, and provided a document that backers could bring to funders in order to demonstrate the high likelihood of both mission and financial success.

CHAPTER 2
GETTING STARTED: DESIGNING AND LAUNCHING YOUR PROCESS

The prospect of a new program, partnership, entity, or growth strategy is exciting, and it can be tempting to jump in and immediately begin researching the market, running numbers, and sketching out how the various parts would fit together. Ultimately, however, this is not the most efficient way to start. It is important to take a small amount of time up front to design a thoughtful process. This is the "D" in the *DARE² Succeed* model.

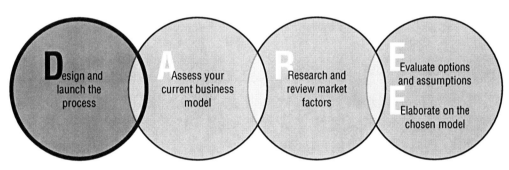

Design and launch the process

Assess your current business model

Research and review market factors

Evaluate options and assumptions

Elaborate on the chosen model

Business Planning: DARE² Succeed

FORMING A PLANNING TEAM

A successful business planning process draws on the expertise of dozens of individuals. The process must be *led* by a much smaller group, however. As consultants, we call this group "the planning team" or sometimes "the business planning committee." It usually includes the CEO and top financial manager (CFO or COO) and sometimes other senior staff or program staff with specialized knowledge of the proposed activity. Depending on a particular organization's size and culture, the planning team may also include board members, middle managers, and/or front-line staff. In a partnership situation, it would typically include representatives from each potential partner or group of partners. If that group does *not* include the future leader of the proposed program, venture, partnership, or entity that is the subject of the business plan (assuming a leader has been selected), it is critical that she or he be included as well—both to include her or his voice in the process and to ensure full understanding of and buy-in to whatever is created.

The ideal size for a planning team is usually between four and ten people. There are exceptions, of course, but, in general, we have found that a very small team does not benefit from the value that can come from including diverse viewpoints, and a very large team can be difficult (and costly) to bring together.

When potential members are invited to participate, they should be told the purpose of the business planning process, the timeframe over which it will unfold, and the approximate weekly or monthly time commitment expected of them. Members should bring a mix of skills and viewpoints to the process. Skills might include experience with financial analysis, knowledge of the program area, or familiarity with key major funders. Member aptitude should include strong strategic thinking, and healthy but constructive skepticism; do not stack the committee with people who are unthinkingly supportive of one course of action, and try to include only people who are able to work well with others.

It is important that the planning team include someone with expertise in financial modeling and experience using financial information to support strategic thinking and decision making. Ideally, this person is the CFO; presumably she knows the organization and its programs well and can participate as a member of the planning team. Alternatively, either a financial professional—whether officially part of the team or not—or a strategy consultant with financial skills can fulfill the role.

Timeframe: The timeframe within which a business planning process takes place varies widely, but, generally, it will be from 10 to 26 weeks in length, allowing adequate time for all required research and financial modeling and for several drafts of the plan to be reviewed and improved upon. Business planning works best when it is an iterative process.

Time Commitment: This is also variable and depends heavily on whether the planning team chooses to engage outside assistance. Even with consulting help, planning team members should be prepared to devote two to four hours a week to the process. Consultants can gather and analyze information, facilitate strategic discussions, prepare financial models, and make recommendations, but, ultimately, they are there to *assist* the planning team, not replace it. The planning team must determine that it has the right information, ensure that the assumptions are reasonable, and recommend (to the CEO or board, as appropriate) final decisions that the organization will be able to implement.

Use Worksheet 1 to help you think through the composition of your planning team.

WORKSHEET 1: FORMING YOUR PLANNING TEAM

In a business planning process, the planning team typically includes the CEO and top financial manager (CFO or COO). It may also include other senior staff or program staff with specialized knowledge of the proposed activity; board members; middle managers; and/or front-line staff. In a partnership situation, it would typically include representatives from each potential partner or group of partners.

Begin by identifying any specific skills, knowledge, experience, or connections you will need, then think about what mix of individuals will best provide those while also working well as a team.

Skills, knowledge, experience or connections desired:

- Financial analysis skills
- Knowledge of organizational structures and systems
- Program knowledge
- Experience with starting / growing organizations

- Strong connections with (select): funders, constituents, partners, potential partners,

  _____
- Other: _____
- Other: _____
- Other: _____

NAME	TITLE /POSITION	SPECIFIC SKILLS, KNOWLEDGE, EXPERTISE AND/OR CONNECTIONS
1.		
2.		
3.		
4.		
5.		
6.		
7.		
8.		
9.		
10.		

The ideal size for a planning team is usually between four and ten people. Fewer than four allows for too few viewpoints; more than ten creates too many process delays.

THE SIX BASIC BUSINESS PLANNING QUESTIONS

Once formed, the planning team should first turn its attention to the six basic business planning questions:

1. What is the *focus* of our business planning effort (e.g., a particular program, a new initiative undertaken either alone or with partners, or the enterprise as a whole)?

2. What is the *strategic intent* of the program, initiative, or enterprise that is the focus of the business planning effort?

3. What *questions* do we need to answer—and what *decisions* do we need to make—in the course of this business planning process?

4. What *information* do we need in order to make these decisions?

5. Who is the *audience* for this business plan, and how will they use it?

6. Who will *approve* the final decisions and document?

Answering these questions at the outset and with as much specificity as possible is essential to focusing the entire process, which can otherwise range far and wide and result in wasted time and energy and a poor outcome.

QUESTION #1: WHAT IS THE FOCUS OF OUR BUSINESS PLANNING EFFORT?

Business planning should not be entered into just because it sounds like a good idea, but rather because there is a specific question (or set of questions) that needs to be answered. It may be undertaken to better understand the economics of a current program, perhaps one that is losing money or, conversely, a programmatically and financially successful program that you hope to grow or replicate. A business planning process may also focus on the organization as a whole, as when you want to better understand overall performance, make adjustments, or prioritize new investments (or cutbacks). Finally, business planning is often used prospectively to structure a new initiative, such as the launch of a program, expansion to a new geographic location, or formation of a partnership with others. In this last case, the business plan becomes a communal document that provides potential partners with a roadmap as they plan for and begin to implement their shared venture. When starting out, be as specific as possible in describing the focus of your business planning effort. For example:

- "The business plan will focus on our child abuse prevention program."

- "The business plan will detail how to incorporate our earned income strategy—establishing a retail outlet for our artists' work—into our overall economic model."

- "The business plan will inform our decision-making process as we consider whether and how to move forward with a partnership with The Science and Technology Center."

QUESTION #2: WHAT IS THE STRATEGIC INTENT OF THE PROGRAM, INITIATIVE, OR ENTERPRISE?

In other words, what are we trying to accomplish? Agreement on this at the outset is essential to ensuring that the business planning process is properly constructed. For example:

- *"The business plan will focus on our child abuse prevention program.* Our intent is to grow the program to become the top provider of child abuse prevention services in our community. We want to offer our proven services to many more families."

- *"The business plan will detail how to incorporate our earned income strategy—a retail outlet for our artists' work—into our overall economic model.* Our intent is to diversify our revenue sources and increase the proportion that comes from earned income while giving our artists additional exposure for their work."

- *"The business plan will inform our decision-making process as we consider whether and how to move forward with a partnership with The Science and Technology Center.* The intent of the partnership is to expand our audience in a sustainable way, reaching an additional 10,000 middle school students annually."

Each of the above descriptions begins with the focus statement and continues with the statement of intent. We continue this pattern below, adding to the summary with each successive question.

QUESTION #3: WHAT QUESTIONS DO WE NEED TO ANSWER—AND WHAT DECISIONS DO WE NEED TO MAKE—IN THE COURSE OF THIS BUSINESS PLANNING PROCESS?

Engaging in business planning is a bit like being an investigator. You have mysteries to solve. Why is this program losing money? What is the best path to growing our services? Will this decision achieve what we intend? Think about your focus and strategic intent and identify the questions you will need to answer through this process. Are you looking for a go/no-go decision on a new initiative? A path to retooling a current program? A more sustainable business model for the entire organization? The critical milestones that will define success in implementation? For example:

- *"The business plan will focus on our child abuse prevention program. Our intent is to grow the program to become the top provider of child abuse prevention services in our community. We want to offer our proven services to many more families.* **We need to determine the best mix of services that will provide both value to the community and a sustainable financial base for us. Our questions include whether we should add, grow, close, or restructure any component of our program and over what period of time."**

- *"The business plan will detail how to incorporate our earned income strategy—establishing a retail outlet for our artists' work—into our overall economic model. Our intent is to diversify our revenue sources and increase the proportion that comes from earned income while giving our artists additional exposure for their work.* **We need to understand more about the market for art sales and analyze both our competition and any opportunities for partnership. We need to know whether projected revenues will be sufficient to make this worthwhile for both our organization and our artists and are likely to be sustainable in the long term."**

- *"The business plan will inform our decision-making process as we consider whether and how to move forward with a partnership with The Science and Technology Center. The intent of the partnership is to expand our audience in a sustainable way, reaching an additional 10,000 middle school students annually.* **To make an informed decision, we need to understand the benefits and risks, the implications for staffing and infrastructure, the capital requirements, and the optimal partnership structure."**

QUESTION #4: WHAT INFORMATION DO WE NEED IN ORDER TO MAKE THESE DECISIONS?

Answering the questions you posed will require some gathering of data. Nonprofit leaders often rely on their gut for decision making. This sometimes works quite well; many leaders are very intuitive and often "guess right" (or seem to). However, when the consequence of being wrong is great harm to the organization, data-based decision making should supplement the leader's gut.

Do you need to project utilization rates and a growth trajectory? You will need information on the demand for a particular product or service and the likelihood that the demand will increase or decrease. Do you need to understand how the timing of necessary investments will impact the likelihood of success? You will need to prepare a financial model looking two to three years out.[6] If the focus of your plan is a partnership, you will probably need recent financial statements for each potential partner in order to do that. Each situation will be different. To continue our previous examples:

- *"The business plan will focus on our child abuse prevention program. Our intent is to grow the program to become the top provider of child abuse prevention services in our community. We want to offer our proven services to many more families. We need to determine the best mix of services that will provide both value to the community and a sustainable financial base for us. Our questions include whether we should add, grow, close, or restructure any component of our program and over what period of time.*

   "We need a three-year financial projection based on three scenarios we'll call aggressive, moderate, and conservative, respectively based on the number of paying clients we think we might attract. We also need to anticipate office-space needs and identify the point at which we will need to add to our infrastructure, for example, by investing in a new technology platform or larger HR department. To answer these questions, we'll need to look at similar organizations that have grown dramatically, examine our own use and cost data over the past five years, and determine whether our board has an appetite for this kind of growth."

- *"The business plan will detail how to incorporate our earned income strategy—establishing a retail outlet for our artists' work—into our overall economic model. Our intent is to diversify our revenue sources and increase the proportion that comes from earned income while*

---

6. We believe financial projections beyond three years to be so unreliable as to do more harm than good because, although they are essentially guesswork, they are often perceived as "fact." It is better to commit to a rolling two- or three-year financial projection than to create a five-year projection today. Financial projections are discussed in more detail in Chapter 5.

giving our artists additional exposure for their work. We need to understand more about the market for this work and analyze both our competition and any opportunities for partnership. We need to know whether projected revenues will be sufficient to make this worthwhile for both our organization and our artists and are likely to be sustainable in the long term.

"To answer these questions we will need to gather and analyze market data (including demand, price sensitivity, competitive offerings, and competitor positioning), create a marketing framework and estimate related costs, understand our own and our artists' cost structure, and develop a pricing model that will build on and support both."

- *"The business plan will inform our decision-making process as we consider whether and how to move forward with a partnership with The Science and Technology Center. The intent of the partnership is to expand our audience in a sustainable way, reaching an additional 10,000 middle school students annually. To make an informed decision, we need to understand the benefits and risks, the implications for staffing and infrastructure, the capital requirements, and the optimal partnership structure.*

"In order to answer these questions we will need to know what programming is most likely to attract middle school students and whether such programming will fill the Center or whether we will have to consider additional target audiences. We need to plan for new staff and understand the partnership's impact on existing staff. We will also need to gather information on the likely cost structure, best practices for structuring partnership agreements of this type, and the impact this relationship might have on our brand."

QUESTION #5: WHO IS THE AUDIENCE FOR THIS BUSINESS PLAN, AND HOW WILL THEY USE IT?

Once the business plan is complete, what will you do with it? Is it designed as a marketing document to give to funders? Or is it a blueprint for staff to follow in the implementation stage? Will it be of use daily in implementation or serve only as a signpost for the metrics of success? Will stakeholders of your potential partner(s) need to see and understand the plan? Are there other stakeholders who will want or need a review? In short, who will read the resulting plan, and what will they do with it? It's worth noting that, when multiple central audiences are identified, the planning team might consider creating supplemental reports or optional appendices that can be left out of some versions; a document designed to attract funding may not contain the same level of detail as an implementation guide, but both may be critical needs. Continuing our examples:

- *"The business plan will focus on our child abuse prevention program. Our intent is to grow the program to become the top provider of child abuse prevention services in our community. We want to offer our proven services to many more families. We need to determine the best mix of services that will provide both value to the community and a sustainable financial base for us. Our questions include whether we should add, grow, close, or restructure any component of our program and over what period of time.*

  "We need a three-year financial projection, program-by-program, based on three sets of assumptions we'll call aggressive, moderate, and conservative, respectively based on the number of paying clients we think we might attract. We also need to anticipate office-space needs and identify the point at which we will need to add to our infrastructure, for example, by investing in a new technology platform or larger HR department. To answer these questions, we'll need to look at similar organizations that have grown dramatically, examine our own use and cost data over the past five years, and determine if our board has an appetite for this kind of growth.

  "This plan will be an important source of data for the CEO and our board as they make resource-allocation decisions in the next year. It will help the board decide where to invest our limited funds for maximum benefit and will guide management's implementation of those decisions."

- *"The business plan will detail how to incorporate our earned income strategy—a retail outlet for our artists' work—into our overall economic model. Our intent is to diversify our revenue sources and increase the proportion that comes from earned income while our artists additional exposure for their work. We need to understand more about the market for this work and analyze both our competition and any opportunities for partnership. We need to know if projected revenues will be sufficient to make this worthwhile for both our organization and our artists and they are likely to be sustainable in the long term.*

  "To answer these questions we will need to gather and analyze market data, understand our and our artists' cost structure, and develop a pricing model that will build on and support both.

  "The plan will be used primarily as an operational guide for staff in implementing this strategy, defining critical action steps, setting opera-

tional and financial milestones, and defining success to ensure we achieve our sustainability goals."

- *"The business plan will inform our decision-making process as we consider whether and how to move forward with a partnership with The Science and Technology Center. The intent of the partnership is to expand our audience in a sustainable way, reaching an additional 10,000 middle school students annually. To make an informed decision, we need to understand the benefits and risks, the implications for staffing and infrastructure, the capital requirements, and the optimal partnership structure.*

"In order to answer these questions we'll need to know what programming is most likely to attract middle-school students and whether such programming will fill the Center or whether we will have to consider additional target audiences. We need to plan for new staff and understand the partnership's impact on existing staff. We will also need to gather information on the likely cost structure, best practices for structuring partnership agreements of this type, and the impact this relationship might have on our brand.

"This plan will be used by both our board and our partner's board to inform the decision of whether to move forward with our joint initiative. It will also be shared with potential funders to show them that we have really thought this through and that this partnership is viable and sustainable."

QUESTION #6: WHO WILL APPROVE THE FINAL DECISIONS AND DOCUMENT?

Finally, you must be clear at the outset as to who will approve the business plan when it is complete. Identify the key decision makers and make sure you understand their concerns and information needs. Be clear on how and when they will be involved in the process and on the method and frequency of communication with them, both individually and collectively.

This is also a good time to identify other individuals whose contributions will be needed throughout the process. Are there particular board members with expertise that could be helpful? Does your Program Director hold a key piece of information? Or is your organizational culture highly participatory, such that staff should be provided with an opportunity to weigh in on central elements of the plan as it evolves? Where in the process will you seek out this input, and how will it be incorporated?

- *"The business plan will focus on our child abuse prevention program. Our intent is to grow the program to become the top provider of child abuse prevention services in our community. We want to offer our proven services to many more families. We need to determine the best mix of services that will provide both value to the community and a sustainable financial base for us. Our questions include whether we should add, grow, close, or restructure any component of our program and over what period of time.*

  "We need a three-year financial projection based on three sets of assumptions we'll call aggressive, moderate, and conservative, respectively based on the number of paying clients we think we might attract. We also need to anticipate office-space needs and identify the point at which we will need to add to our infrastructure, for example, by investing in a new technology platform or larger HR department. To answer these questions, we'll need to look at similar organizations that have grown dramatically, examine our own use and cost data over the past five years, and determine whether our board has an appetite for this kind of growth.

  "This plan will be an important source of data for the CEO and our board as they make resource-allocation decisions in the next year. It will help the board decide where to invest our limited funds for maximum benefit and will guide management's implementation of those decisions.

  "The CEO will determine whether to act on the recommendations of the business plan, working in consultation with the Program Director and subject to the board's budgetary approval. Two representatives from the board are serving on the planning team; they will provide regular updates to the full board. The board will also have an opportunity to review the draft plan toward the end of the process."

- *"The business plan will detail how to incorporate our earned income strategy—a retail outlet for our artists' work—into our overall economic model. Our intent is to diversify our revenue sources and increase the proportion that comes from earned income while giving our artists additional exposure for their work. We need to understand more about the market for this work and analyze both our competition and any opportunities for partnership. We need to know whether projected revenues will be sufficient to make this worthwhile for both our organization and our artists and are likely to be sustainable in the long term.*

  "To answer these questions, we will need to gather and analyze market data, understand our and our artists' cost structure, and develop a pricing model that will build on and support both.

  "The plan will be used primarily as an operational guide for staff in

implementing this strategy, defining critical action steps, setting operational and financial milestones, and defining success to assure we achieve our sustainability goals.

"The board will make the final go/no-go decision based on the plan presented. The plan itself will be approved and then implemented by the CEO and Center Manager. Since this represents a vital strategy for organizational sustainability, the Center Manager and CEO will report quarterly to the board on program and financial milestones."

- *"The business plan will inform our decision-making process as we consider whether and how to move forward with a partnership with The Science and Technology Center. The intent of the partnership is to expand our audience in a sustainable way, reaching an additional 10,000 middle school students annually. To make an informed decision, we need to understand the benefits and risks, the implications for staffing and infrastructure, the capital requirements, and the optimal partnership structure.*

  "In order to answer these questions, we'll need to know what programming is most likely to attract middle school students and whether such programming will fill the Center or whether we will have to consider additional target audiences. We need to plan for new staff and understand the partnership's impact on existing staff. We will also need to gather information on the likely cost structure, best practices for structuring partnership agreements of this type, and the impact this relationship might have on our brand.

  "This plan will be used by both our board and our partner's board to inform the decision of whether to move forward with our joint initiative. It will also be shared with potential funders to show them that we have really thought this through and that this partnership is viable and sustainable.

  "The plan will be adopted or rejected by our board and our partner's board as part of a decision to move forward with the partnership. Representatives of each board are serving on the planning team; throughout the process, these individuals will facilitate information flow and provide introductions to other board members or stakeholders who might have relevant expertise or information."

As you can see, in answering these six basic questions (reiterated in Discussion Guide 1), you have created a framework that will drive the business planning process, give it focus, save time, and, if you are working with consultants, enable you to launch the engagement with a common understanding of where you are heading.

DISCUSSION GUIDE 1:
SIX BASIC BUSINESS PLANNING QUESTIONS

Discuss the following questions with members of the planning team, conferring with other stakeholders as necessary. Compile your answers into a short summary that can serve as a reference document for all involved.

 What is the focus of our business planning effort (e.g., a particular program, a new initiative undertaken either alone or with partners, or the enterprise as a whole)?

 What is the strategic intent of the program, initiative, or enterprise that is the focus of the business planning effort?

 What questions do we need to answer—and what decisions do we need to make—in the course of this business planning process?

 What information do we need in order to make these decisions?

 Who is the audience for this business plan, and how will they use it?

 Who will approve the final decisions and document?

CASE STUDY: KNOWLEDGE FORCE – PART 1

Amy Rivera had been the Executive Director of Knowledge Force for three years. Although it was not a large organization, Knowledge Force had developed an award-winning program that trained volunteers to be school-based tutors. With a $3.2 million budget, it was several times larger than the local tutoring organization she had previously led.

Knowledge Force had built its evidence-based programs over 15 years by focusing on students in kindergarten through third grade, with an emphasis on those at risk for falling behind grade level. It was founded by two talented, retired teachers who realized that their network of colleagues was also retiring from teaching, and, like them, these dedicated professionals were still interested in being engaged with their communities. The founders built the organization over ten years, developing curricula, leveraging their relationships with colleagues, learning how to fundraise, and establishing the program in a handful of metropolitan areas. In the beginning, they began soliciting volunteers through retired-educator networks, and, by the time Amy came to the organization, nearly 75% of the volunteers were retirees. After ten years on the job, both founders retired within a year of each other.

The Knowledge Force model was heavily dependent on volunteers, each of whom worked in the classroom with small groups of children. Since finding volunteer tutors is a decidedly local business, the organization had built a national presence by establishing local offices; it now had operations in eight metropolitan areas. Each locality, typically staffed by a Program Manager and a Program Assistant, was responsible for the whole array of programming: cultivating school relationships, recruiting and training volunteers, and reaching out to local funders. The national office, based in Washington, DC, provided the curriculum, supported training and fundraising efforts, coordinated program evaluation, and provided all administrative support, including human resources and IT services.

In her first three years as Executive Director, Amy had focused on stabilizing the organization. Following the retirement of the founders, Knowledge Force had hired an Executive Director, who pursued an aggressive expansion policy. Within his first year on the job, he had opened offices in four new metropolitan areas, bringing the total to ten. Two years later, the organization found itself running a significant deficit and operating with too few human resources nationally. The Executive Director left, and Amy took over an organization in desperate need of change. Her initial priorities were to cultivate local funders in the strongest of the new regions, terminate programs in two underperforming areas, secure the organization's first grants from major national funders, and support her board as it moved from being an educator-based group to a fundraising body. Amy's move to shut down two sites was unpopular among staff and some board members—but it had also left an impression of her as a leader willing to make tough decisions. Amy was proud of the work she had done to stabilize the organization and build a positive balance sheet but was also frustrated that she had spent so much time retrenching rather than pursuing any new initiatives. First things first.

Now things were looking up. Knowledge Force was poised to end the current year with a surplus of about $200,000, or 6% of expenses, contributing to the reserves it had struggled to build, and next year's budget looked stronger still. A dynamic new Development Director had begun to expand the organization's national fundraising capacity, putting in place an aggressive program of individual and major donor solicitation that was ready to ramp up dramatically. And two months previously, an unexpected bequest arrived: $250,000 now to be followed by a smaller amount when the estate proceedings were completed. Amy had fully supported the board's decision to reserve the bequest for one-time projects; she hoped it would be seed money for a more reasonable expansion.

After 20 years in the education field, Amy knew without a doubt that the Knowledge Force model worked. She had first worked with Knowledge Force staff when she was a teacher and had stayed in touch with the national leadership during the years before she came on board. While a teacher, she had participated in a university evaluation of the program that had shown a substantial increase in literacy among Knowledge Force students compared with those in other tutoring programs. Not content to rely on one study, Knowledge Force, in partnership with a nearby university and with foundation support, had invested in periodic evaluations through the years, resulting in an evolving approach to both training and tutoring that consistently proved effective. The benefit extended beyond students: two studies had shown that retirees participating as volunteers had seen improved quality of life. Knowledge Force's commitment to improvement and proof of its value through multiple studies led to receipt of several national and local awards for educational and civic excellence.

When talking with funders, Amy described Knowledge Force's vision for eradicating childhood illiteracy one city, one school, one volunteer, one student at a time. She knew it was time to take Knowledge Force to scale.

Knowing that the organization's previous major expansion effort had had the perverse effect of stalling growth for several years, Amy was determined to avoid the same mistakes. She had spoken many times with her immediate past Board Chair, Thomas Johnson, about expanding. Thomas was a retired Senior Vice President of a large national foundation and, while with the foundation, had provided critical support during the establishment and early growth of Knowledge Force. Having retired, he joined the Knowledge Force board just as the previous Executive Director had left. Although initially skeptical of Amy's ability to work on a national level, he had become her strongest ally, serving as a close advisor during her first year as she analyzed the organization's position and spearheaded closure of the weakest expansion sites.

He had subsequently led the board's change process, rallying members to shift their focus and learn how to become effective fundraisers. Many evenings during the first year, Amy had left the office whispering a little word of thanks that Thomas was there to introduce her to his national funder network, push the board forward, and identify potential new board members.

In the early days, when Amy began to think the organization might need to retrench, it was Thomas who asked her to put together a financial analysis that communicated the need for such a drastic step. More recently, when Amy talked about expanding Knowledge Force's reach, Thomas again asked for details. He emphasized that he needed to know two things: the financial proposition and the implications for mission advancement. The financial piece was about data: how much would it cost and how would Knowledge Force pay for it? With respect to the mission, Thomas wanted to know how the organization would support expansion in a way that kept its focus firmly on increasing literacy.

STARTING OUT

Amy knew she needed a business plan to answer Thomas's—and her own—questions, so she and Thomas brought to the board a proposal to create a board/staff planning team, hire a consultant, and engage in a business planning process. The board, excited to be considering expansion once again, readily approved the plan, allocated funding for the process, and asked Amy to create the working committee.

Amy and Thomas had already talked about who should be on the planning team, and Amy had prepared a short paragraph outlining team-member expectations, so she was ready the next day to speak with each of the individuals on the list.

Amy knew she must have Thomas on the team because he was both her closest advisor on the board and a hard-nosed, data-oriented thinker. Her Program Director and CFO were essential as well. She wanted one more board member but was uncertain who would best move the process forward. In many ways, Amy knew that the board member best suited to this kind of process was Sofia Grandison, but Amy had never really liked her much. Sofia was a manager at a textbook-publishing company and seemed to have little understanding of how a nonprofit operated differently from a business. Sofia spoke without inhibition, which grated on Amy in every meeting, but the sharpness was regularly cut with incisive observations and good advice. Sofia had told Amy she was interested in participating, and keeping her involved wouldn't hurt their chances of succeeding in their current effort to double Sofia's employer's annual contribution.

After talking through her options with Board President Maria Fernandez, Amy asked the four to serve. After some questions about expectations, they all agreed to participate on the planning team:

- Amy Rivera, Chair
- Henry Jiang, Program Director
- Deborah Robinson, CFO
- Thomas Johnson, board member
- Sofia Grandison, board member

The planning team met for the first time shortly thereafter. Amy suggested they start by discussing two fundamental questions:

- What do we want to accomplish in this effort?
- What will be the process for moving forward? (e.g., timeline, hiring of a consultant)

The questions prompted a lively conversation and detailed discussion of several different viewpoints, but, in the end, the team agreed on the basic goals and process elements. These were consolidated over the next several days into the following project scope:

This business planning process—and the plan that emerges—will be used primarily as a decision-making tool. It will guide us as we determine the feasibility and scope of further expansion. Secondarily, it will map out the implementation steps needed if we move forward.

Through expansion, we intend to increase literacy rates among children in each community we work in, and we will ultimately increase national literacy.

The primary decisions we need to make are whether to move forward with expansion and if we do, where and how quickly. Our specific questions are:

- What capacity (staffing and infrastructure) will we need for expansion?
- What will expansion cost?
- Can we secure the resources for expansion? Will funders be interested in supporting our expansion?
- How do we expand so that our skills, success rate, and brand are both leveraged and protected?
- If we move forward, what will be the major implementation steps for successful expansion?
- What are the implications for governance and for the role of the board (and individual board members) if we expand?
- What are the implications for national-office staffing or operational needs if we expand?

In order to answer the last question on the list, we explicitly need to know:

- What is our current capacity? (Do we have the skills and infrastructure needed for our current workload? For our potential future workload?)
- Can we scale our systems and increase our efficiency sufficiently to support a larger organization?

Consistent with our primary purpose of using this effort to inform our decision-making process, the primary audience for any product or report will be the Board of Directors. The secondary audience will be the managers, who (assuming we move forward) would use it as a starting point for implementation. Although we are writing this to guide us internally, a business plan will aid us in talking with funders and other external audiences.

The critical decision about moving forward with expansion will remain the board's, although any detailed questions about how to do so will remain with the CEO, subject to the board's budgetary authority.

At the first meeting, the planning team also agreed to issue an RFP to hire a business planning consultant. Amy asked Thomas to work with her in hiring the consultant and also to seek capacity-building funding from a national foundation to support the effort. After speaking with several consultants and reviewing many proposals, Amy hired Sharon Raymond to work on the project along with the planning team. Sharon was a senior manager with a small national consulting firm that specialized in nonprofit work. What appealed to Amy was that Sharon's primary practice was in strategy development but, as a former nonprofit CFO and Executive Director, she brought strengths in financial analysis and organizational development, as well as a keen awareness of the cultural implications of an undertaking like this.

Within a week of Sharon's hiring, the team gathered for their second full meeting. She facilitated and, working from the previously prepared project scope, asked questions designed to dive more deeply into the rationale behind the idea of expansion. By the end of the session, the group was able to summarize their discussions and next steps as follows:

QUESTION: WHAT NEED WOULD THE EXPANSION MEET?

DISCUSSION: The primary purpose of an expansion would be to increase literacy among low-income students (K-3). A secondary purpose would be to improve the quality of life for volunteers. A key consideration would be to avoid expansion that led to duplication (i.e., Knowledge Force might not seek expansion to a given community if good programs or alternatives were already present there).

WORK PLAN: Conduct research to identify regions with the highest poverty/lowest literacy rates among K-3 students. Conduct research to identify regions with high populations of retirees. Correlate the two to identify possible target areas for expansion, and research existing programs in those areas.

QUESTION: IS THE NEED GROWING?

(e.g., numbers of low-income, low literacy children)

DISCUSSION: Henry had broad demographic data at his fingertips—he had used it repeatedly in grant applications—describing both rates of childhood poverty and educational outcomes for all metropolitan areas in the country. The information he had gathered (from the census bureau, the Department of Education, and other sources) included both recent surveys and anticipated growth in different factors.

WORK PLAN: No new research needed, but the business plan will need to capture and build on this information.

QUESTION: WHAT TRENDS IN THE ENVIRONMENT MIGHT IMPACT THE NEED?

DISCUSSION: At first, the planning team thought this question had been covered in the discussion of demographics. But, as they carried the conversation forward, Thomas remarked on how many of his former foundation colleagues were talking about cuts to their education portfolios in favor of protecting the foundation's job readiness efforts with young adults and the unemployed. This could mean the loss of funding for similar programs or supports for Knowledge Force's target audience.

WORK PLAN: Survey foundations in the targeted communities to better understand their plans for youth/education funding.

Sharon concluded the meeting with a conversation about the role of the planning team members and her role as consultant. She summarized their agreements as follows:

Sharon:
- Design overall process and structure for the business plan, with full input from team
- Serve as primary author for the business plan, working closely with Amy and incorporating major sections written by team members
- Act as "second" for all research
- Support ongoing communication with staff and board around process and progress
- Challenge assumptions

Planning Team Members:
- Provide input into process, business plan design, and business plan content
- Fulfill primary responsibility for conducting market research and drafting related content, including gathering data about metropolitan demographics and trends in the field (Henry) and seeking information about funding trends and foundation interests (Amy, working with the Development Director)
- Deborah: take the lead in developing financial models, working closely with Amy and Sharon, and utilizing Sharon's analytical tools
- Amy: responsible for ongoing communication with staff, including solicitation of input as needed
- Amy, Sofia, and Thomas: responsible for ongoing communication with the board, including solicitation of input as needed

CHAPTER 3:
ASSESSING YOUR CURRENT BUSINESS MODEL

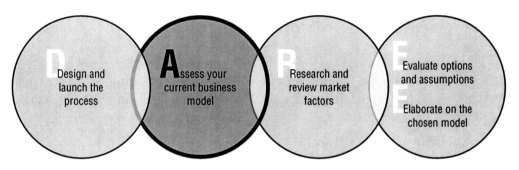

Business Planning: DARE² Succeed

The second step in our *DARE² Succeed* model is to assess your current business model. Done well, the business planning process examines and either validates or suggests changes to a nonprofit's current business model. Thus, except in the case of a completely new initiative, it is best to begin a business planning effort by assessing the health of the current business model. Doing so will yield valuable information that can (and should) inform both the business planning process and the resulting plan. Even if you *are* preparing a business plan for a completely new initiative, we suggest you read on: the principles put forth in this section will help you think about how to build a healthy business model from the outset.

Often when we hear someone say "We need a new business model" or "Our business model is broken," what he really seems to be saying is "We need more revenue" or "We can't seem to make ends meet." This results from looking at the economic logic of a program or organization in isolation. As referenced in Chapter 1, our earlier book *The Nonprofit Strategy Revolution* defined a nonprofit business model as the interplay of the organization's scope (geographic, programmatic, and customer) with its economic logic (how it structures and pays for itself).[7] This more inclusive definition can become the basis for assessing the health of your current business model.

---

7. The treatment of business model here is necessarily brief. For a fuller description of how to define your business model, see *The Nonprofit Strategy Revolution*.

- Geographic Scope—where do we do our work?
- Programmatic Scope—what do we offer?
- Customer Scope—whom do we serve?
- Economic Logic—how do we structure it financially?

Although you may not have thought of it in these terms, your organization has always had a business model that consciously or unconsciously operates in certain geographies and not in others, provides some services or activities and not others, and serves some customers, clients, or constituents while ignoring others. You also have a budget that matches revenues to expenses, or at least tries to. The "broken" part of an ailing business model may lie in any one of these areas, or in several. Deconstructing the business model into these elements allows you to analyze what part is working well, and what is not. This should be a primary focus for the planning team early in the business planning process.

After examining the organization's scope (geographic, programmatic, and customer) and economic logic, the planning team should step back and evaluate the business model through one additional lens: overall organizational capacity. Is there an infrastructure in place sufficient to support the current business model or, more important, the business model you are considering? If not, what changes will be needed if the program, venture, partnership, or entity you are describing is to be successful?

Figure C: Understanding and Assessing
Your Business Model

STEP 1: EXAMINE YOUR SCOPE

To assess the health of your current business model, begin by describing your *current* geographic, programmatic, and customer scope and what has worked well about that focus. Then think about what might *not* be working optimally in each area. You may find it helpful to use a grid like the one in Discussion Guide 2 to organize your responses.[8] Sample responses are shown in Figure D.

8. For more on understanding and describing your business model, see *The Nonprofit Strategy Revolution*, pages 51-52.

DISCUSSION GUIDE 2: EXAMINING YOUR SCOPE

	Geographic Scope	Programmatic Scope	Customer Scope
Current profile			
Strengths of your current profile			
Shortcomings or deficiencies in your current profile			
If you could make one change in this dimension of your business model, what would it be?			

DISCUSSION GUIDE 2: EXAMINING YOUR SCOPE
Ourtown Film Festival

	Geographic Scope	Programmatic Scope	Customer Scope
Current profile	Our mid-size city and surrounding communities The two nearest big cities (each within a three-hour drive)	Film screening (at least one per month) Two 2-day events (a summer film festival, an autumn industry gathering) School outreach program	People of all ages interested in film (film other than Hollywood blockbusters) Filmmakers and the film industry (non-Hollywood)
Strengths of your current profile	Our focus "fits" with the image our community tries to cultivate; both big cities have strong film communities and many wealthy prospective donors	High ticket sales indicate this seems to be working	Our non-Hollywood focus also fits with the culture of the community
Shortcomings or deficiencies in your current profile	We would like to start reaching out to the online community of cinephiles, but we haven't done a great job at establishing a robust online presence		We haven't had any luck attracting college students, despite repeated outreach efforts
If you could make one change in this dimension of your business model, what would it be?	Reach beyond our immediate geographic area by increasing our online presence	We thought about accepting submissions for the film festival (rather than an invitation-only system), but that would be too labor-intensive at this point	Stop focusing on college students and on tourists; put our resources and efforts into the over-40s, families with kids, schools, and young professionals (as well as filmmakers and the film industry)

Figure D: Sample Responses for Ourtown Film Festival

Note that, in this example, the summary analysis of Ourtown Film Festival led to a strategic decision: to refocus the organization's attention away from college youth and tourists to others. It is not unusual for an analysis of the business model to result in the need for a new organizational strategy intended to address a weakness.

STEP 2: ASSESS YOUR ECONOMIC LOGIC

Once you have considered and discussed what is working (and not) vis-à-vis your scope, it is time to take stock of your economic logic—specifically, your funding and finances.

A comprehensive financial assessment should look at the following:

1. **Surpluses.** Generating consistent year-over-year operating surpluses is a key indicator of financial strength. Since nonprofits do not have shareholders to whom "profits" are distributed, any surplus that is generated will need to be reinvested in the organization to support its mission or held to promote sustainability by strengthening its cash position. Whether surpluses are used (e.g., for program expansion) or set aside (e.g., for a building reserve, opportunity fund, rainy-day fund, etc.) is a strategic decision that the organization's leadership must clearly understand. Consistent deficits are often an indicator of structural deficiencies (deficiencies that will continue to exist even when things are otherwise going well) with the current business model.

2. **Reliability of Revenue.** Reliability of significant revenue sources is critical and correlates with the sustainability of the economic model. It is important in any financial assessment to arrive at a shared understanding of which sources are reliable and which are uncertain in the short and long term.

3. **Costs and Cost Allocation.** Identifying direct program costs and using a well-defined and consistent methodology to allocate shared costs ensures that the fully loaded costs of programs are identified and funded. If this isn't something your organization has done to date, now would be a good time to start. Failure to fully understand, appropriately apportion, and secure funds to cover shared costs is a major reason for nonprofit financial failure.

4. **Structure of Assets.** Organizations can be categorized into those that are facility intensive—requiring specialized and therefore expensive space in which to deliver their services (theaters, hospitals, schools, and the like)— and those that are not. For the former, there are often significant costs associated with facility management (e.g., fixed-asset replacement, upgrades, debt service, facility reserves) to consider when assessing financial risk. Facility-intensive organizations are also at risk of seeing the value of their properties drop due to factors outside of their control, such as a downturn in the real estate market. Organizations that are *not* facility-intensive need to carefully examine the assets they do have (e.g., receivables, cash reserves, an endowment) and consider how future plans and

goals may change or put stress on the current structure of the balance sheet. It is also important to assess whether your assets are structured to support your organization over time. For example, is your building a revenue-generating asset, and/or is it central to service delivery?

5. **Liabilities.** Debt is not necessarily a four-letter word. A line of credit, for example, is an appropriate tool for managing cash flow challenges. A mortgage makes sense if a building is core to the business model or if ownership costs are less than the cost of a lease. It is essential to assess whether an organization's debt has been used for the right reasons (e.g., for the acquisition of an asset such as a building or for short-term cash flow management) vs. the wrong reasons (e.g., to plug recurring operating deficits) and is manageable from a budgetary standpoint. It is also important to examine the rates and terms of any debt, especially in the new environment of more-stringent bank covenants, and carefully consider the downside or risk of over-leveraging. A nonprofit that has increasing payables and/or debt as a result of repeated deficits should flag this as a risk. High payroll tax liabilities caused by delay in payment of these taxes should be considered a risk because it may indicate the organization has used the taxes withheld from employees for operations. (Don't underestimate the seriousness of this particular red flag. The IRS doesn't take this lightly and *will* collect—if not from your organization, then directly from board members, insurance notwithstanding.)

6. **Liquidity and Reserves.** It is critical to have sufficient cash on hand to manage cash flow. It is also important to hold reserves sufficient to address fixed-asset upgrades or replacements and manage other external risk factors, including the risks associated with a new venture or a financial downturn. In fact, one specific measure of liquidity, unrestricted liquid net assets, is sometimes referred to as an organization's risk reserve. Auditors' reports often call this out. It can also be computed using data from your balance sheet: take your unrestricted net assets and subtract out buildings, land, and other property, net of accumulated depreciation, and any related debt.

Reserve requirements will vary depending on subsector and business model. Broadly speaking, three to six months of operating expenses held in liquid reserves is a minimum prudent standard. However, each organization must define for itself what constitutes an appropriate reserve. The amount will be influenced by the leadership's overall tolerance for risk as well as its assessment of the risk associated with the proposed program, venture, partnership, or growth strategy. While there is no right answer *per se,* you may want to consider the following:

- How many months of operating expenses can your current risk reserve cover?
- Have your financial projections[9] factored in the need to grow your risk reserve at a rate commensurate with growth of your operating budget?
- What opportunities exist to increase your risk reserve (e.g., liquidate an asset, fundraise, etc.)?
- How strong is your monthly cash inflow? If you predictably receive a steady flow of income, you may be comfortable with a smaller reserve than if your income arrives unpredictably.

A BIT OF ADVICE

There are several caveats to be aware of when calculating the risk reserve. First, if your organization has borrowed against the market value of a building, it may distort the results of the risk reserve calculation since buildings are booked on your balance sheet at cost, when in fact the building may be worth significantly more or less in today's market. Additionally, there may be legitimate reasons to carve out portions of your overall reserve and consider them "unavailable," such as when establishing a building reserve. These considerations should all be discussed with your CFO, Finance Committee, and/or auditor and eventually factored into your financial plan.

Discussion Guide 3 provides a starting point for a conversation about your economic logic, during which you can identify any areas where you might be at financial risk. Where you do identify challenges or risk factors, consider how these might impact the likelihood of success for your new program, venture, partnership, or growth strategy, and how you might address or mitigate them as you move through the planning process.

9. Financial projections are discussed in more detail in Chapter 6.

DISCUSSION GUIDE 3: ASSESSING FINANCIAL RISK

Members of the planning team—together with the CFO, Board Treasurer, and/or members of the Board Finance Committee, if possible—should review the organization's history and performance in each of the six areas listed below. For each, identify areas where the organization has performed well and areas where it has struggled or might be at some financial risk. Be sure to link your discussions back to the business planning process; think about how each of the strengths and challenges you identify will impact how you go about launching your new venture or how each might impact your chances for success. What could you do going forward to lesson your financial risk?

Consider:

Surpluses

Reliability of Revenue

Costs and Cost Allocation

Structure of Assets

Liabilities

Liquidity and Reserves

Where are we strong?

Where are we struggling? Where might we be at risk?

How will we acknowledge, leverage, and/or address these strengths and risk factors in the business planning process?

STEP 3: EVALUATE YOUR ORGANIZATIONAL CAPACITY

Finally, think broadly about what is working—and not working—in your organization now. Are you wrestling with human resources issues? Wanting but not attracting positive media attention for your work? Constantly struggling to support sky's-the-limit mission delivery with bare-bones infrastructure? If you run multiple programs now, what characterizes those that are most successful? What characterizes your most successful staff teams or, if you are looking at a partnership opportunity, your organization's most successful partnerships? Think about how each of the strengths and challenges you identify will impact how you go about launching your new venture or how each might impact your chances for success. (Discussion Guide 4 provides a list of areas to consider.) Make note of anything you will need to consider further in the planning process or address specifically in your plan.

It can be hard for those working within an organization to be fully honest (even with themselves) about its situation. Because of this, many nonprofits find that it helps to get an outside perspective on the organization's strengths, weaknesses, assets, and liabilities, through interviews, focus groups, or formal assessments. Whatever you choose to do, keep your end goal in mind, identifying those factors that are most likely to affect the success of your proposed program, venture, partnership, or growth strategy or influence how it is structured.

> It can be hard for those working within an organization to be fully honest (even with themselves) about its strengths, weaknesses, assets, and liabilities. Because of this, it is helpful to get an outside perspective.

DISCUSSION GUIDE 4: ORGANIZATIONAL STRENGTHS AND WEAKNESSES

Begin by discussing the following questions with the planning team. Consider each area listed in the first box below. Decide together the extent to which you would benefit from soliciting additional opinions, for example, from other members of the board and staff, clients/customers, organizational partners, or funders. Be sure to link your discussions back to the business planning process; think about how each of the strengths and challenges you identity will impact how you go about launching your new venture, or how each might impact your chances for success.

Consider:

Programs/Services Provided	Funding/Fund Development
Staffing/Workforce	Marketing and Communications
Leadership	Reputation and Brand Recognition
Governance	Organizational Culture
Financial Management	Influence
Contracts/Contract Management/Compliance	Facilities
Cultural Competency	Purchasing
Information Technology	Partnerships
Human Resources	Mission-related Impact

 What is working well? Where are we strong?

 What is not working well? Where are we struggling?

 How will we acknowledge, leverage, and/or address these strengths and challenges in the business planning process?

BUSINESS PLANNING FOR A NEW VENTURE

When business planning is undertaken to better understand, improve, grow, or build on an existing organization or program, you begin the process with extensive data. You know, for example, that, for the past five years, the program has served on average 100 patrons a day or that the required staffing cannot be lowered beyond a certain number without creating serious quality or security concerns. Your current business model may be ailing, but at least you usually have, or can get, the information needed to make a sound diagnosis. This is not necessarily the case when you undertake business planning to assess the feasibility of a new or substantially new undertaking. Such situations typically require more effort to gather and analyze the type of information needed if you are to be as thorough in the process—and confident in the result—as would be the case with an ongoing venture.

Approaches to gathering and working with data in this situation include the following:

LOOK FOR EXISTING MODELS. Look for others who have done what you propose to do elsewhere. In Chapter 1, we described a proposed partnership among a group of organizations—some public, some private, some nonprofit—to launch an energy retrofit program for low-income households. In this case, the planning team looked to a handful of other cities around the country that had launched similar initiatives. The structures were different, but the core work was similar, and the variety of financing options used was enlightening.

LOOK FOR ANALOGUES. Study similar or analogous ventures or organizational structures. You may not have undertaken this activity before, but it is likely someone has tried something similar, albeit in a different field, community, or context. For example, the national animal-welfare group merging with local affiliates could look to a multi-party merger in another field or could research governance, staffing, and cost structures for other national organizations. The field may be substantially different, but the lessons learned about working across organizations and sectors may well be applicable.

CONSIDER OPTIONS FOR PARTNERSHIP. For an entirely new initiative, develop and evaluate different scenarios for how the launch might play out and consider partnership as one option, rather than starting from scratch. A team developing a new program to combat homelessness, for example, could model what it would cost to launch the program independently, in collaboration with an existing organization, or by using a local organization's facilities. As you gather more information, you will be able to select among or merge elements of the various scenarios into your final plan.[10]

10. For more on scenario planning, see *What If? The Art of Scenario Thinking for Nonprofits*, by Diana Scearce, Katherine Fulton, and the Global Business Network community. http://www.gbn.com/articles/pdfs/GBN_What%20If.pdf

CASE STUDY: KNOWLEDGE FORCE – PART 2

Sharon wanted to understand more about what had contributed to Knowledge Force's financial difficulties the last time it had tried to expand; she approached Deborah, the CFO, with her questions. Deborah led finance discussions at the board level and served as a partner with program staff in creating grant proposals; she understood the strengths and weaknesses of each group. In the course of their discussion, Sharon learned that Amy was highly skilled in finance. Other members of the planning team, however, *felt* they had a good understanding of Knowledge Force's current financial position, but several didn't understand it as well as they thought. Deborah expressed frustration that the board often didn't incorporate thoughtful financial analysis into its strategic decision making, although they clearly understood the need for it in this process. Given what she learned, Sharon suggested a session in which the planning team would review the organization's financial history and current situation. A shared understanding of both would be important going forward, and what the group learned would inform the strategic decisions currently under consideration. Deborah and Amy agreed; together they prepared an analysis and walked the team through the findings.

Everyone knew that Knowledge Force had a history of running deficits, a trend that had reversed only in the two most recent years. Although the planning team was aware that the deficits were correlated to unsuccessful expansion, it was helpful to revisit the key lesson learned from that experience: it was incredibly risky to expand without securing up-front capital to support the agency through its growing pains. Knowledge Force had assumed that revenues would materialize more quickly than they actually did.

Historically, Knowledge Force had generated revenues from a variety of sources, some more reliable than others. Large national grants came in periodically and were usually designated as seed funding for expansion efforts rather than ongoing operations. Overall, Knowledge Force was highly dependent on local sources of funding. School revenues, for example, were a critical source of revenue for several of the most financially healthy sites, supplemented by local foundation and individual support; however, other sites were not able to persuade local school districts to pay for tutoring services. These sites struggled and survived only by cobbling together various grants from local foundations, corporations, and a handful of individuals. Deborah was able to describe how even the most successful expansion sites required a steady source of revenue. Based on what she saw there, Deborah believed that school revenues had to be an essential part of a viable growth plan.

Deborah reviewed the financial performance of each of the current sites, demonstrating how the two most financially successful had been able to secure between $15,000 and $25,000 in revenue for each school they served. Because a single Knowledge Force site could serve multiple districts, each with multiple schools, these revenues would add up quickly. Deborah noted that the successful sites covered not only the direct costs of the site itself but also the portion of indirect costs from the national office that had been allocated to them. This allocation had been an ongoing source of tension within the organization; regional managers often complained that they were expected to raise funds for their site *and* cover a portion of the costs associated with the national office. More than once, Deborah had taken pains to explain that the national office was responsible for raising the national dollars that supported each of the sites, not to mention paying for the administrative, curricular, and other technical support that each site relied upon. She knew quite well that any expansion plan would need to consider the fully loaded cost of establishing a new site (including additional costs for the national office) and to ensure viable, sustainable revenue sources adequate to cover all of these new costs—not just in the short term but also for the long haul.

Knowledge Force did not own any buildings; its programmatic work occurred in schools, and it generally subleased its regional office space, which consisted of no more than a room and a desk, from other nonprofits. Its balance sheet consisted mostly of cash and receivables with some fixed assets in the form of furniture and equipment. Aside from a national-office lease in Washington, DC, and a lease on a copier in that office, it had no debt or liabilities to speak of. Still, Deborah's analysis showed how prior-year deficits had eaten up nearly all of the cash reserves that had been accumulated in the past. In spite of the recent year's surplus, reserves barely covered two months' worth of expenses. "If we try to grow again with this balance sheet," said Deborah, "we'll end up broke. We need capital to expand; otherwise, we will put the whole organization at risk."

CHAPTER 4
RESEARCHING YOUR MARKET

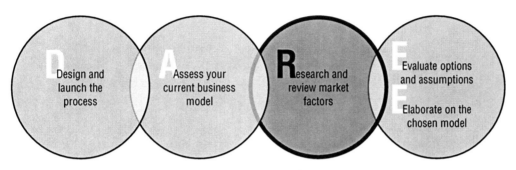

Business Planning: DARE² Succeed

The third step in the *DARE² Succeed* model is to research and review market research. Market research is an important tool for answering the critical questions that come up in a business planning process: What is the need for the product or service you are proposing? What is the competitive landscape within which you will be operating?

Determining need is a fairly straightforward and necessary step when you are planning a new program, new venture, or growth strategy. Whether you will be working alone or in partnership with another organization, there is no sense to starting or expanding a program or service that serves a nonexistent or shrinking need. If you *are* considering a partnership, you and your partner should discuss the needs that each is striving to meet, quantify those needs, and determine how the partnership will enable you to better address those needs together. Even if the primary motivation for the partnership is to achieve administrative efficiencies and economies of scale, you still must know—and show—that there is a true need for what the consolidated organization will bring to society.

> **Proper planning requires an early focus on two things: the need for the product or service you are proposing, and the competitive landscape.**

The text box below lists some of the key questions that the planning team should consider when defining and quantifying the need for the product or service under consideration.

QUESTIONS TO CONSIDER

Defining and Quantifying the Need for Your Product/Service

- What need will your product/service meet?

- How do you know the need exists?

- Is that need growing, shrinking, or staying the same?

- What trends in the environment might impact the need? (e.g., rising unemployment is likely to lead to an increase in homelessness; more adults with health insurance will increase traffic at community clinics)

- Is each identified trend likely to continue, accelerate, decelerate, or reverse? Over what time span and to what degree?

- How would you define your target audience or client/customer base for the service? Whose need(s) are you meeting?

- How large is the potential audience or client/customer base? (Quantify to the best of your ability.)

- Is the size of the target audience or client/customer base growing, shrinking, or staying the same? Is that likely to continue, or change? Over what timeframe and to what degree?

Nonprofit organizations operate in a competitive environment. They compete for resources of all types—funding, clients, staff, volunteers, board members, media attention, and relationships with key influencers. It is critical to understand where the proposed program, venture, partnership, or expanded organization sits in the competitive landscape. You will need resources to implement whatever it is you are planning; why should those resources be directed to your organization and not to one of the many others working in the same or a similar space? What is your competitive advantage, the visible, obvious and measurable way(s) in which your organization differs from and is better than its peers?

The following text box lists some of the key questions that the planning team should consider.

QUESTIONS TO CONSIDER

Competitive Landscape

- How else could your clients/customers/audiences get these needs met? Consider direct, substitutable, and resource competitors.[11]

- Which would you consider to be your top three to five competitors?

- Where is each of the identified competitors strong? How do they—or will they—compare with the organization you are describing? (By this, we mean either your existing organization, after implementation of your proposed program or growth strategy; the consolidated organization, after a partnership; or the new organization, if you plan to create one.)

- Have you identified needs that are not currently met by any other organization or competitor?

- What is (or will be) your organization's competitive advantage? Why is what you are proposing so compelling, even in a crowded competitive landscape?

- How will you maintain this competitive advantage? Will your competitors attempt to duplicate that which currently sets you apart? If so, how could you respond?

- How would you summarize your value proposition, the benefit that you will deliver and the client/customer/audience member will experience?

How should you go about doing market research? The method used and the level of detail sought will depend on your situation. In general, however, you will want to employ some combination of secondary and primary research. Secondary research draws on data and materials that already exist and have already been gathered, analyzed, or made public for another purpose. Some of this may be internal to your organization: demographic information on your current clients/customers/audience, for example, or the results of client satisfaction surveys. Other sources of secondary data are external to

11. Direct competitors are organizations with the same market focus; organizations that do what you do, within the same geographic area, for the same types of customers. Substitutable competitors are organizations that meet the same need that you do but in a different way. Indirect competitors are organizations that do not compete with you for customers but do compete for other resources such as funding, board members, and staff. Source: *Play To Win: The Nonprofit Guide to Competitive Strategy*, by David La Piana with Michaela Hayes, page 93.

your organization: existing market studies, census data, competitor websites, trade publications, etc. Primary research is tailored to your specific needs and conducted specifically on your behalf. Primary research techniques include interviews, focus groups, direct observation, and surveys. Generally, it is most economical to do secondary research first and then use primary research to build on and contextualize what you learn.

Following are tips specific to some of the most common market research techniques:

- **Secondary research.** The Internet is a great place to start. Look for demographic information, economic forecasts, and articles or blog posts about trends in the sector and in your field. Check out the website of each of your competitors. Review agendas, presentations, and proceedings documents from recent conferences focused on content areas relevant to what you are proposing. Identify key players or "thought leaders" that might be able to shed light on market trends or the strengths and challenges of the various players in your field.

- **Interviews.** Talk with current clients or customers or review customer-needs surveys and find out how they perceive the value of what you offer now and what you are planning to offer in the future. Identify other key stakeholders who might help you understand the competitive landscape and your place in it or who might choose (or not) to support your program, venture, partnership, or growth strategy. Interview one or more "thought leaders" in your field or representatives from other organizations that have gone through a process similar to what you are proposing. What did they learn from their experience that might inform yours?

- **Focus groups.** Sometimes, it can be helpful to engage a group of stakeholders in a conversation about an organization or concept, particularly when you need to understand perceptions about something you are currently doing and/or interest in and response to something you are considering doing in the future. Focus groups can be done with customers, clients, employees, volunteers, or even board members from the organizations that would be involved in the program, venture, or partnership. Skilled organization and facilitation is needed to get the most out of the experience; be sure to engage a trained moderator who can effectively distill the results into usable intelligence. While focus groups are traditionally done in person, they may also be facilitated over the phone and online.

- **Surveys.** Surveys can be another valuable source of information. Through a series of carefully thought-out questions, you can gather a large number of opinions on everything from unmet needs to perceptions, beliefs, and attitudes about your organization and your competitors, to the likelihood that someone would avail themselves of a particular program, service, or opportunity. Surveys can be paper-based, conducted online, or conducted via telephone. Survey design is an art; be sure to run your questions by multiple people (including some with relevant experience) before you finalize them. Keep it short; people are inundated with surveys these days, and you don't want to irritate those from whom you are seeking input. Consider some kind of incentive: response rates tend to go up when a carrot is attached!

Not all business planning processes will devote equal attention to market research. For some, it will be critical. A new theater, for example, should be considered only after the planning team has a thorough understanding of the market and is able to make detailed projections about audience, membership, and the size and characteristics of the potential donor base. In other situations, launching into a detailed examination of the need for your product or service would be, if not a *waste* of time, at least less than crucial. For example, a national organization with 12 affiliates might be considering merging all of them into one unified entity. Each individual corporation may have current data on market demand and projected service volume for its geographic area, all of which has been incorporated into its current financial projections. At the same time, the planning team might have significant questions about the ability of the merged entity to truly coordinate its efforts, take advantage of economies of scale, and provide an infrastructure able to effectively launch and support the types of national initiatives not fully possible within the current, more fragmented structure. In this case, less time would be spent on market research and more on infrastructure development.

Regardless of the depth of the research or the methods used, the planning team should take time to sift through what it does learn as a group and discuss the implications for the design of the strategy in question. If adjustments to the concept are made, the group should determine whether any additional research is needed to test the revised concept. Continue with this process until you are confident that you understand—and can describe—a compelling need, a strong demand, and a competitive position worthy of further investment.

CASE STUDY: KNOWLEDGE FORCE – PART 3

Over the course of several weeks, Henry had conducted preliminary research to identify metropolitan areas with high poverty, low literacy rates, and high numbers of retirees. He had shared his findings with Amy and Sharon, who passed the information along to the other members of the team along with a question: should Knowledge Force focus on expanding into new metropolitan areas or on deepening its presence in currently served areas? Either option could result in Knowledge Force's reaching more children, but organizational needs and risk, not to mention the potential for nationwide impact, might differ in each scenario.

After discussing the initial research, the planning team decided to take a closer look at ten metropolitan areas: five new, along with the five currently served areas where Knowledge Force had a presence but relatively low market penetration. Since the team already knew that each of the ten had passed the first screen (being high poverty with low childhood literacy and high numbers of retirees), Sharon urged the group to identify other organizations focused on literacy in each area. By the end of the meeting, the planning team had agreed on the critical next step: Sharon would work with Henry to create an analysis of the competition in each area. Over the next few weeks, the pair identified all of the organizations providing tutoring to low-income children in each target area and then narrowed their list to the three or four that were most similar to Knowledge Force. They sent the planning team ten charts (one for each target area) that looked like the following:

	For-profit ABC	Local Nonprofit QRS	Nonprofit XYZ
Overview of Programs/ Services	Serves K-12 Serves both low-income students through school contracts and paying students through parent payment	Serves K-5 Program built around paying parents to engage in after-school learning activities with children	Serves K-5 Hires tutors from all facets of community, usually individuals seeking extra income Approach built around strong methodology similar to KF
Geographic Focus	National chain operated through local franchises	Only City X	National, with greatest presence in the Southwest
Client/Constituent Focus	Recent graduates Public brand/ communication aimed at both the upper middle class (parents able to pay) and school districts	Parents	Schools and administrators
Primary Funding Sources	100% fee-driven, paid by both schools and individual families	Individual contributions Major local institutional funder provides 30% of budget	School contracts
Key Strengths and Points of Differentiation	High cachet by hiring only young adults with advanced degrees to provide tutoring services	Grassroots base among parents Local knowledge	Strong presence among educators; close relationships with school administrators; strong marketing presence in education conferences and journals
Service Gap (needs they are not meeting)	Limited ability to contract with schools because of high-cost model	No consistent methodology beyond parent involvement Results not independently evaluated	Unknown
Our (potential) Competitive Advantage in This Market	Relationship with retirees, many of whom are former teachers Evaluated methodology Low-cost model subsidized by independent funders		

At its next meeting, the planning team reviewed the competitor research and created a summary analysis identifying several strengths or competitive advantages that Knowledge Force could leverage in any new community. Amy then distributed the background materials and the planning team's analysis to the full board as well as to the rest of the management team and added a discussion of both to the agenda for the next board meeting.

That discussion took place several weeks later and was both spirited and productive. By the end of the board meeting, the group had posited that Knowledge Force's critical competitive advantages were:

- A methodology that is proven to be superior for improving K-3 literacy
- Strong skills in attracting retirees as tutors
- Low per-student cost as compared to other providers

"But that first competitive advantage really worries me," said Amy at the end of the discussion. "Is there really a 'secret sauce,' or could anyone take a look at what we do and build a similarly effective program? I learned from the Knowledge Force curriculum when I ran a tutoring program, and I know others have done the same."

"I sometimes wonder about that myself," Maria, the board chair, responded, and several board members' heads nodded agreement.

Henry responded, "I think the methodology is important, and, while it's not rocket science, it is more fully developed and consistently up-to-date than any of our competitors' products."

Sharon helped clarify: "It will continue to be important to keep that edge if Knowledge Force is going to sustain this competitive advantage, and it's only an advantage to you if people know about it, so you need to brand and promote the unique aspects of your approach."

After the board meeting, Sharon identified two critical next steps: the proposed competitive advantages needed to be confirmed (Henry's assurances were helpful but not enough), and the planning team needed to narrow the list of potential expansion areas. It tackled both issues at its next meeting. Drawing on input from other managers, the group identified a dozen external stakeholders who knew the organization and field well, including several funders, a former manager who had gone to work for another tutoring organization, and various school personnel who had recently considered contracting with both Knowledge Force and competing services. Interviews with these individuals would serve to "test" the validity of the competitive advantages. While the planning team discussed splitting up the list and having each member interview two or three people, they decided in the end to have Sharon interview everyone, believing that the feedback would be more balanced if provided confidentially to an independent consultant.

After finalizing the plan for stakeholder interviews, the team turned to the question of how to narrow the list of potential expansion areas. There was still much they needed to understand about costs and risks in order to choose between a focus on new or existing metropolitan areas, but that would come later. They decided to focus the next level of research and planning on three possible locations in each of the two categories.

Although Amy believed she already knew which communities to keep in the mix, Sharon insisted that they take a few minutes to identify their selection criteria. "The criteria have been implicit since my first conversation with you," Sharon noted, "but making them explicit will keep us grounded, and it will also leave you with a useful tool for future discussions." Together, they drafted the following screen:

We will prioritize expansion where:
- *The need is high (defined by high numbers of children living in poverty and low literacy rates)*
- *The population of retirees is high*
- *We can leverage our competitive advantages, as demonstrated through competitor research*
- *We can identify funders to support our expansion*

The fourth point was added based on lessons learned from the previous expansion effort. It also served as a placeholder of sorts: if the potential for local revenue appeared strong, expansion into that area was more likely to be affordable. Actual costs—which would inform the final decision—would be described later.

Amy was gratified that the planning team's conversation, rooted in the selection criteria, led to the results that she had expected. But she also saw how the members of the strategy team began to use the language about competitive advantage and mission impact to justify their choices. As she watched Henry and Sofia engage in the conversation, she saw their excitement for the potential grow. She knew that they would both be much stronger advocates for whatever direction the planning process indicated than if she had simply announced the decision to expand.

Throughout the course of the conversation, the planning team created several charts to aid their comparative thinking. Following is a sample:

	Option A	Option B
Poverty Rates & Literacy Rates	One of the highest poverty rates in the country, high illiteracy	Lower but still relatively high poverty rates and higher income disparity; slightly less illiteracy
Senior Population	A bit lower as a percentage of total population than the national average	One of the highest retiree populations in the country
Competitive Advantage: Methodology	Only local tutoring groups in the market, none using evaluated methodologies	Several groups using evaluated methodologies in the market, including Amy's former organization
Competitive Advantage: Attracting Retirees	No local knowledge of retiree population	No local knowledge of retiree population
Identified Funders	Two major statewide foundations supporting KF work already; local foundations small; minimal wealth leaders in community	Few high-funded local or statewide foundations and Knowledge Force has no relationship with any; several high-wealth community leaders

At the end of the conversation, they had tentatively decided to consider Dallas, Baltimore, and Phoenix as the test cases for expansion into new metropolitan regions, pending further research. Using a similar discussion guide, they prioritized Detroit, Cleveland, and Memphis for expansion within a currently served region.

CHAPTER 5
DEVELOPING YOUR PLAN

At this point in the process, you should have a good grasp of your current business model—including those elements that might need to change—and of the market in which you will be operating. It is now time to dive more deeply into actual planning. This is the "E" in the *DARE² Succeed* model: *evaluate* different options and assumptions in order to reach agreement on a favored model and then *elaborate* on that model.

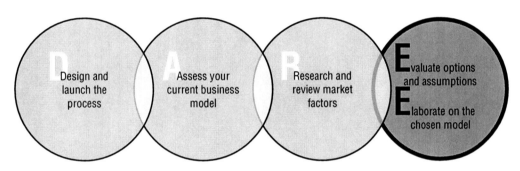

Business Planning: DARE² Succeed

This phase of work involves considering such questions as:

- What will operations and infrastructure look like post-launch?
- How will the program/partnership/entity be managed and governed?
- What collaborative relationships will be important?
- What will be the overall marketing strategy?
- What will revenues and expenses look like, and what capital investment will be required?
- How will you evaluate and measure impact?

Keep in mind that good business planning does not proceed in a linear fashion but is instead an iterative process. You will need to pose questions, answer them tentatively, test your answers, move on, and then cycle back—possibly more than once.

THE TABLE OF CONTENTS AS A PLANNING TOOL

In Chapters 2 and 3, we identified the first steps in the business planning process, which included convening a planning team and identifying the purpose for engaging in business planning. We have found it helpful to translate that purpose into an outline or draft "table of contents" for the plan you hope to create. (An example is shown in Figure E.) This may seem a bit premature, but, in practice, starting out with a clear sense of where you hope to end up is extremely helpful. It serves to get everyone on the same page—literally. Even if you are working on your own, sketching out at the beginning what the final document will include (at the level of section headings) will help your team agree on your destination and help surface and resolve any differences of opinion. This initial table of contents is not carved in stone; you will likely make changes to it as the process unfolds.

Executive Summary

Mission, Vision, and Desired Impact

The Program, Organization, or Initiative
- History
- Current/Future Business Model
- Programmatic Focus

The Market
- Market Trends
- Market Needs
- Market Segmentation
- Competitors
- Positioning Statement

Management and Operations
- Governance and Management
- Organizational Structure and Staffing
- Operations and Infrastructure
- Volunteer Engagement

Key Collaborative Relationships/Partnership Model (if a partnership)

Marketing Strategy

Financial Projections and Fund Development
- Financial Assumptions
- Capitalization Strategy
- Fund Development

Evaluation and Measurement of Impact

Risks and Risk Mitigation

Appendices

Figure E: Sample Business Plan Table of Contents

Every process—and every resulting business plan—is different. The content of your plan will depend heavily on your goals and your audience. If you are trying to demonstrate that there is, in fact, a real need for the very new and unique program, product, or service you are proposing, you may choose to focus heavily on a discussion of the market and on your marketing strategy. If you are trying to persuade funders and stakeholders that you can implement a complex concept successfully, you may choose to focus more on structure, infrastructure investments, staff expertise, and timeline. If you are trying to confirm the sustainability of your idea, you may focus most diligently on detailed assumptions and revenue projections.

OPERATIONS AND INFRASTRUCTURE

You've clarified your strategic intent and identified—at least in broad strokes—how you are going to get there. You've done your market research, gained an understanding of your target audience, tested your concept with stakeholders, and defined your competitive advantage. Now it's time to think about how to operationalize what you want to do. Here is where the concept of an iterative process really comes in. As you begin to define—and later *refine*—the specifics of your program design, staffing structure, administrative functions, etc., you will need to attach estimates for associated costs and revenues. Very likely, you will find that you can't afford everything you'd like to do—at least initially. So, go back to the drawing board. Be as realistic as possible about what it will take to execute successfully. For example, an inadequate financial management system isn't just a nuisance when you're planning to scale up operations twenty-fold or seek out government funding for the first time; it could lead to disaster. Likewise, planning for rapid hiring of front-line staff without putting in place an adequate supervisory structure could cause your entire program model to collapse.

When thinking about how to operationalize your program, venture, partnership, or growth strategy, pay attention to each of the following:

- Program(s) and Services: Your Mechanism(s) for Mission Delivery
- Marketing and Communication
- Information Technology
- Human Resources
- Financial Management
- Fund Development
- Volunteer Engagement (if appropriate)

For each area, think about how you would define your vision for the future as well as the staffing and structure required. Identify any high-priority implementation tasks and timeline considerations and any major costs associated with what you are proposing.

QUESTIONS TO CONSIDER

Operations and Infrastructure for Each Area:

- What is your vision for the future?
- What kind of staffing will be required?
- What are the structural implications?
- What are the highest-priority implementation tasks?
- What are the most important timeline considerations?
- What are the major costs associated with what you are describing?

For example, the aforementioned national organization with 12 affiliates that is considering merging all of them into one unified entity might begin to summarize its conclusions with the following:

	Vision for the Future	Staffing and Structure
Program	Integrated national structure	Visionary national Program Director
Marketing and Communications	Consistent national brand that allows for local variation	• Consultant to design • Coordinator on staff to implement with local staff
Information Technology	• Unified system that facilitates/encourages information sharing • Strong online/social-media presence	• Consultant to design • New media expert on staff • National IT strategy with local tech-support staff
Human Resources	• All staff employed by unified entity • Standard structure and benefits	Experienced HR Director
Financial Management	• Timely reports for national and local management • Regular and robust contribution to strategic conversations and program evaluation	(New) CFO position
Fund Development	Leverage stronger national presence; seek out national foundations and corporate funders	Expertise/relationships either in the Director of Development or through an experienced consultant
Volunteer Engagement	• Local capacity to leverage volunteer services • Volunteer input into national activities	Coordinate with support of new-media expert

Additional detail on vision, staffing, and structure—along with identification of implementation tasks and timeline considerations—would be provided either in the body of the plan or in an appendix and related expenses incorporated into the financial model. This organization's planning team, for example, might declare as its vision that all staff will be employed by the national organization and work within a standardized human resources structure with regard to compensation, benefits, professional development, and performance management. Thus, it will be critical to identify and hire a seasoned Director of Human Resources as soon as possible after the decision to merge. There are costs associated with both the position and the search process, and they must be included in the *"pro forma"* budget. (*Pro forma* financial statements—including a forward-looking statement of revenue and expenses, referred to here as a multi-year budget—are those prepared in advance of an anticipated transaction or business model change to preview the likely financial impact of that change.)[12]

On a smaller scale, the tutoring program we've been following may decide that its vision for the information-technology function is that all tutors have real-time access to information on their students' progress as well as resources and best practices for improving their craft. If student data are not currently available to tutors in electronic form, the organization may need to invest in a robust and secure database system able to support the size and scope of the program envisioned. Although it may not be possible to know the exact cost of developing and implementing such a system at this stage, an estimate should be made and included in the financial projections.

One of the outcomes of this stage of the process should be an organizational chart (often referred to as an org chart or organigram): a graphic representation of the relationships among the various positions and people in the organization. This should be included in the business plan.

12. http://en.wikipedia.org/wiki/Pro_forma

ASSESSING THE IMPACT OF A NEW PROGRAM ON AN EXISTING ORGANIZATION

One of the most difficult aspects of business planning for a new program is reliably predicting the impact of that program on your existing organization.[13] Although any significant change or expansion will affect your current activities, a wholly new venture, not operationally tied to your current activities, is more likely to challenge assumptions about your mission, values, and reputation. To some degree, the relative scale of the new undertaking is an indicator for internal impact: if the new initiative will grow the overall organization by only 10%, its impacts may not be that different from the kind of impacts you would experience with your normal organic growth rate. However, if the new venture represents a substantial amount of growth (we have seen everything from 50% to 500%), you may have to think about fundamentally reinventing the organization, with new layers of management, new IT systems, reconsidered mission statement, or expanded communications or HR capacity. You will also need to build an intentional change management process into your implementation plans.

There is another dynamic at play when considering the impact of substantial growth on your current operations. Nonprofits may grow programmatically along a more or less steady arc, say, 3%-10% a year on average over many years, but infrastructure is created in steep stairsteps because each improvement requires substantial new investments in people and technology.

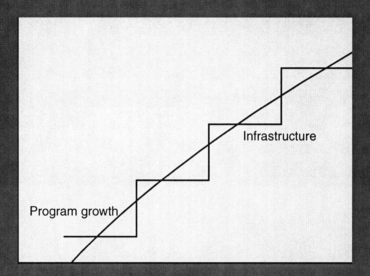

Moreover, in our experience, there appear to be certain budget sizes where these infrastructure investments are especially painful. For example:

The first and most basic shift a growing nonprofit goes through is when it evolves from a volunteer

---

13. If the new venture is an entirely new organization, the planning team will need to do additional work around establishing a corporate entity, forming a board of directors, and setting up basic organizational functions and policies.

movement to one with paid staff. New legal requirements, new risks, the shifting role of the board, and the emergence of a board-staff dynamic—even if there is only one employee—fundamentally alter the organization.

For staffed organizations, the next big hurdle comes when the Executive Director is no longer responsible for program delivery as well as management. At some point in every growing organization's life, it will decide it needs to hire a Program Director (or Chief Operating Officer) who will lead the organization's work while the Executive Director devotes his or her efforts to strategy, management, board development, external relationships, and fundraising. This point is often reached as the budget approaches $1 million.

As the organization grows, it adds systems to manage a growing staff, more-sophisticated finances, diversified fundraising, and the need for more-sophisticated information technology. We have observed a phenomenon we call "$3 million hell." At a certain point, around $3 million in annual expenses, the organization's management needs become sufficiently complex to require a large step-up in systems. Perhaps it needs a full-time Chief Financial Officer or a major investment in IT. But, at $3 million, it cannot afford these infrastructure investments. In fact, business planning is often undertaken at this point because of frustration over insufficient management and inadequate systems. Our advice: try to grow through this stage as quickly as possible. $4 million-$5 million will be a more comfortable place— for a time.

Another break point for organizational infrastructure is when the organization moves from one office or service-delivery site to two. Many experienced executives have found that growing from one location to two was far more difficult than growing from, for example, seven sites to ten. Organizational culture is fundamentally altered when all staff members no longer work from the same location.

CASE STUDY: KNOWLEDGE FORCE – PART 4

For some time during this process, Amy and Henry had been having side conversations about the relative benefits of expanding to reach more youth and shoring up their current capacity. The two had worked hard in the current budget cycle to find funding to expand administrative and training capacity at the national office, and Henry was especially concerned that a major expansion would overstress their current capacity and make it difficult to maintain consistent program quality. Amy knew it was time to open up the discussion and engage in some deeper thinking with her management team. They had been kept up-to-date on the planning team's progress all along, but now she needed their hands-on experience to inform the discussion. She, Henry, and Deborah convened a working session with Henry's two Regional Directors and the Development Director, with Sharon facilitating.

"We have to think about what in the organization would need to change in order for expansion to succeed," Amy explained at the beginning of the meeting. "What sort of resource growth will be needed to support the kind of program growth we're looking at? What systems and skill sets will we need? And what will we need to do to make sure we don't undermine the great work we're doing already?"

Julianne, who oversaw the western region, jumped right in. "You've all heard me say this a million times. We need to standardize our approach to working with school districts. We need to have a contractual template that tells me what's negotiable and what's not. Every time I raise this, we all say, 'Yes, yes, we'll do that,' but we never get around to it. I can't manage two or three more sites, each with multiple school districts, where I have to go back and decide once again what we will and will not do in each of these one-off agreements every time the smallest question is raised."

Deborah jumped in: "There will always be variation in the contracts; the districts won't sign without that. What we need is a good database that makes it easy to access the relevant information quickly—and compare how the agreements differ."

Marco, Manager for the eastern region, reacted to that. "But, if we're going to start spending new money, it shouldn't be in hardware. We should invest in people. I can help the program staff, but I'm not the best trainer, and I keep stumbling across ways that people are doing things differently—and wrong! We need a really good trainer who knows how to distill the essence of our approach down to key lessons and hit on them hard. That will make us better right off the bat. Each school will operate with more consistency, especially in applying what's most important to our success. Our students will learn more!"

"That is absolutely right," agreed Olivia, the Development Director. "I can ask funders for program expansion, but getting funds for IT investment is a lot harder. What funders *really* like—and never want to pay for—is our evaluation data. Can't we find a way to build in a certain percentage of all revenue for evaluation? It really gives us an edge compared with other literacy programs."

The conversation went on this way for two hours while Sharon pressed to understand the various needs and to capture them all on flip charts. After each participant voiced his or her concerns and suggested priorities for investment, the group explored each need and discussed how each would change with growth. Under Sharon's guidance, they began to identify issues they had not thought through previously—such as telecommunications costs and travel—and to prioritize the organization-wide, or "enterprise," needs with one eye toward the budget.

By the end of the meeting, they had identified three specific investments that would be critical if Knowledge Force were to grow as envisioned:

- Increased programmatic support from the national office, including evaluation expertise, curriculum development, and training
- Regionally deployed fund-development staff
- More capacity to establish, build, and maintain relationships with individual school districts

The first time the last point was raised it seemed out of context for several in the group. They didn't think they could expect new local staff to foster still-better relationships with their partners. But, after some discussion about Thomas's door-opener role with foundations, they began to see that it was not just possible for the local staff to be relationship managers within their districts; it was imperative.

"Our business is inherently local," Olivia, the Development Director, reminded the group. "If individual schools and districts don't want to work with Knowledge Force, then there is no business."

Henry agreed. "We need two skill sets: door-openers and relationship managers. A door-opener would be a big shot who's well-known in our circles, like Maria, who's been recognized as one of the best school superintendents in the country. Someone who worked in a school as a principal or superintendent and can speak to his or her peers *as* peers. This type of person could serve either on the board or on a local advisory committee."

"Right now," Marco added, "our relationship managers are the local Program Managers, but they have all they can handle managing existing relationships and supervising staff." This insight led to a thorough discussion of how Knowledge Force could support the local Program Managers differently to help them be more effective. What was needed was a combination of more national support around training, curriculum, and contracting, and additional local staffing once five school districts or ten schools were operated out of a single office.

The meeting ended with Sharon and Henry scheduling a follow-up session during which they would create a complete staffing plan for a growth scenario that would include both national staffing needs at different levels of growth and also local-office-staffing needs, taking into account typical staff-to-school ratios. This information would be essential for understanding the relative advantages of the two growth options (growing in current regions vs. expanding into new metropolitan areas). It would also be critical to understanding staffing and infrastructure needs and planning for the costs of expansion.

GOVERNANCE AND MANAGEMENT

Pick up any article or book on business planning for *for*-profits, and you'll find some variation of the following:

> *A good leader can make a success of a weak business plan, but a poor leader can ruin even the best plan.*

> *A mediocre plan well implemented will outperform the most brilliant plan accompanied by mediocre implementation.*

Both statements are 100% true in the nonprofit sector just as in the corporate world. The single most important factor in a venture's success is its leadership. For nonprofits, this means having an engaged, effective board of directors and a skilled leader (or better still, a skilled management team) at the staff level. No matter how complete or compelling, a written plan lacks a dynamic element capable of adjustment, a critical skill that leadership must provide. It is talented leadership that motivates others to carry out the plan, fills in the pieces not spelled out in the plan, makes changes as new information comes available in a dynamic environment, and serves as a spokesperson to garner resources. As General Eisenhower, the great planner of the D-Day invasion, once said, "In preparing for battle, I have always found that plans are useless, but planning is indispensable."[14] He meant that his battles, like yours, will be won by well-prepared people, not by the plans that helped prepare them, which often must change or might even be abandoned in the course of action.

Very likely, you have already identified at least the primary staff leader for the program, venture, partnership, or growth initiative that is the focus of your

14. www.quotationspage.com/quote/36892.html

business plan. Perhaps it is your current CEO or an outstanding program manager currently working in another part of the organization. Perhaps it is a well-respected manager from your partner's senior leadership team or a team made up of the Executive Directors of each of the partnering organizations. Don't rush into a decision; take the time to make sure there is a good fit between the person or team chosen and the very complex work ahead. Not every executive is a good fit for the unique work of launching a new venture or taking an organization through a massive growth process. Keep in mind that, for very large initiatives or complex organizations, you'll want to fully describe the staffing not just at the chief-executive level but at least one level below as well.

Once your team is identified, it will be important to name its members and describe their skills and qualifications in the business plan. This is particularly true if you expect to be sharing your plan with potential funders or investors. They will absolutely want to know that their investment is in good hands. The bigger the investment, the more a concern this will be. Note that many venture capitalists base their investment decisions first and foremost on the quality of the management team that will lead the venture. Similarly, foundation leaders will sometimes acknowledge that, for large grants, they are more interested in the confidence they feel in the leader than in the quality of the proposal. Make sure you have the right people leading your effort.

If you *don't* feel you have the right person or team on board, identify the qualities you are looking for and define a search process. Be clear on who will be leading implementation in the meantime. Never underestimate the importance of leadership; it will be one of the most important things you address in your plan.

QUESTIONS TO CONSIDER

Governance and Management

- Who will lead the program, partnership, new venture, or expanded organization described in the business plan?

- For each person identified, why is this person the right choice for the position? What skills, experience, and/or perspective does s/he bring? Has she or he successfully implemented something like this before?

- For each position yet to be filled, what kind of individual are you seeking? When and how will the search process proceed? Who will be handling those responsibilities in the meantime?

- What role will the board, the board chair, and/or other individual board members play?

CASE STUDY: KNOWLEDGE FORCE – PART 5

The planning team, led by Sharon and with support from staff, continued to gather and analyze the information it identified as necessary to the planning process. As they moved forward, Sharon reminded them of their early conversations about the audience for the business plan. While the plan was primarily intended to assist the board in making decisions about expansion and to guide the management team in executing those decisions, it was highly likely that potential funders would request a copy, and, even if they didn't, Amy would want them to have one. If Knowledge Force chose to expand, the document must clearly demonstrate to a reader who had not been involved in its creation that expansion was a good idea, and that a significantly larger Knowledge Force was economically and operationally viable and positioned to have the greatest possible impact.

"Although we continue to conduct research and are engaging in rigorous financial analysis," Sharon explained to the planning team at one point, "many believe that the single most important factor in a venture's success is its leadership. The business plan must include at least a short section on who is going to bring this strategy to life. The plan is, after all, just a blueprint, and it will need continual refinement once you begin implementation. You need to tell potential funders or partners why this group of individuals will succeed." To that end, Amy drafted the following for the team to review:

The Knowledge Force Team is led by CEO Amy Rivera. Amy has worked in education her entire professional career: she spent 13 years teaching elementary school in Tucson before being hired as Executive Director of Southwestern Tutorial. While leading Southwestern, she doubled the budget and expanded the organization to new areas of Arizona and into Nevada. She was hired as the Knowledge Force Executive Director three years ago and, in that time, has increased the budget by 25%, moved operations into a surplus, and added new academic partners for program evaluation. Amy received both her B.A. and Master's in Education at University of Arizona at Tucson.

Program Director Henry Jiang received his Ph.D. at Stanford University School of Education and stayed on as an Assistant Professor for four years. Seeking more hands-on work with at-risk students, he became an elementary school teacher in the Ravenswood School District in East Palo Alto, CA, while maintaining part-time status at Stanford. He came to Knowledge Force eight years ago and has served as the Program Director ever since, leveraging his academic relationships to bring rigorous independent evaluation to the Knowledge Force methodology.

Deborah Robinson, CFO, received both her undergraduate degree in Business

Administration and her Master's in Financial Analysis from the University of San Francisco. After working for several small businesses in the San Francisco area, she sought out more meaningful work in the nonprofit sector. She joined Knowledge Force ten years ago as a Program Assistant in the Oakland Metro office. Her aptitude for business and financial skills were quickly noted, and Knowledge Force supported her to return to USF to pursue her Master's in Financial Analysis, which she was awarded six years ago. Following graduation, she was promoted to Administrative Coordinator in the national office and then to CFO three years later.

Olivia Ryan, Development Director, has been with Knowledge Force for just over one year. With 11 years' experience leading development efforts at nonprofits with budgets between $5 million and $15 million, Deborah has brought considerable energy and insight to the development function at Knowledge Force. In one year, she has both expanded the organization's national fundraising capacity and put in place an aggressive program of individual and major donor solicitation that is poised to ramp up dramatically.

Board President Maria Fernandez is the retired Superintendent of Schools in Phoenix. She previously served as Superintendent in Riverside, CA, and Albuquerque, NM. Although she began her career as a teacher, she became particularly interested in learning methodologies and spent five years pursuing her Ph.D. in Education and five more as an Associate Professor of Education at the University of Arizona in Tucson specializing in childhood learning and program evaluation.

Although not ready to commit to a change just yet, Amy recognized that Henry's responsibilities could grow considerably if Knowledge Force pursued an aggressive growth plan—and that his title would need to reflect that.

KEY COLLABORATIVE RELATIONSHIPS

Even in cases where the focus of your business plan is not a formal partnership, it is quite likely that successful execution will require working closely with others in the field. A theater group might be dependent on its landlord at a performing arts center, for example, or a social-services provider dependent on local-government contracts. More broadly, nonprofits are operating in an increasingly complex environment, taking on increasingly complex issues; it is the rare nonprofit that won't find its success at least somewhat dependent on its ability to leverage and work with networks, groups of people and organizations (formal and informal) working together to achieve a larger goal. The planning team should identify the collaborative relationships that will be most important going forward, and articulate how each will contribute to the success of the venture that is the focus of the business plan. If there are several partners to consider or if these relationships are particularly complex, it may be necessary to put in place structures, systems, or staff to support them.

SIGNIFICANT PARTNERS

If the focus of your business plan *is* a formal partnership—an administrative consolidation, joint program, merger, parent-subsidiary relationship, or jointly formed new entity, for example—you will need to describe how the relationship will operate and determine how it will be structured. Will it be governed by a contract or memorandum of understanding (MOU)? Will leadership be shared or designated to one or a subset of the partners? Will the partnering organizations legally merge or retain separate corporate structures? If merging, how will members of the merged entity's board be selected? If multiple organizations are coming together to launch a new organization, will the "founders" have any rights or responsibilities that future partners, if they emerge, will not be offered?

Partnerships are unique; defining the terms usually requires a negotiation process. Negotiation typically covers many topics. You won't need to include every decision or detail in the business plan, but make sure you include the highlights. Again, consider your audience: if you are trying to demonstrate to key decision makers or potential funders that you've covered your bases and are poised for success, include enough information to make that clear.

QUESTIONS TO CONSIDER

Key Collaborative Relationships

- Who are our past and current collaborators? Are there other organizations in our region or field with which we might collaborate in the future?

- How do we—and will we—communicate with and learn from others in our field?

- Does our pursuit of this program, partnership, venture, or growth strategy present any opportunities to deepen our collaboration with others?

- Are there ways to better engage our network(s) as we go forward, and in so doing, increase our impact?

CASE STUDY: KNOWLEDGE FORCE – PART 6

In the course of conducting the competitor analysis, Amy and Thomas had been struck by the strength XYZ Tutorial brought to its relationships with schools. XYZ's Executive Director had been an Undersecretary at the U.S. Department of Education. Two of its board members had been Secretary of Education at the state level, one in Texas and the other in Missouri. XYZ's staff included longtime teachers and administrators. Amy saw them at every educational conference she attended, front and center with their materials, hosting receptions and participating on panels.

Sharon urged the planning team to consider XYZ's strong competitive position as they moved forward, and recommended that Knowledge Force focus on strengthening its local school connections as part of any growth plan. Amy wasn't convinced that doing so would make that much difference, certainly not in the next few years. "We'll never compete with them!" Sofia had blurted out at the board meeting where the group discussed competitor research. "We should just let them take us over."

At the time, Amy had inhaled deeply and pushed aside her irritation. The concept of merger had not been on the agenda, but now that someone had broached the topic it needed to be addressed. Other board members chimed in, some saying that it made no sense at all to merge and others stating that it made all the sense in the world. Eventually, the conversation moved on without any clear resolution. But, after the meeting, the thought kept coming back to Amy: was merger a good option? She knew XYZ was strong in Texas and a few nearby states where Knowledge Force had no presence. She was critical of their curriculum but thought they were well-organized. And their marketing and outreach were second to none.

As the strategy team reviewed and discussed its recommendations for prioritizing communities for expansion, they decided to include a partnership with XYZ—possibly in Philadelphia, a promising location where neither XYZ nor Knowledge Force currently had a presence—as one avenue to explore. Engaging in an initial discussion would allow Amy and Knowledge Force to learn whether XYZ was open to curricular changes based on Knowledge Force's model but would also help Knowledge Force by bolstering key relationships in the field. In time, Amy could imagine a nationwide partnership or even a merger, but, for now, the team focused on the first step only, which was to schedule a meeting between the CEOs and Board Presidents of each organization to discuss a partnership involving "neutral turf."

MARKETING STRATEGY

While many nonprofits have a built-in client or customer base (a food pantry in an economically depressed community usually has no trouble finding families to whom it can distribute groceries, for example), it is still necessary to define a value proposition and communicate that to potential clients, customers, funders, and the community as a whole. This process falls under marketing, the official definition of which is the activity, set of institutions, and processes for creating, communicating, delivering, and exchanging offerings that have value for customers, clients, partners, and society at large.[15] Articulating a strategy for marketing and outreach, even at just the highest level, is an important step in the business planning process.

Some organizations think of marketing as a "business" concept applicable primarily to for-profits, but understanding and being able to articulate the following is as important for nonprofits as it is for corporations:

- The specifics of your product(s) and/or service(s), and your competitive advantage: Why is what you are proposing so compelling, even in a crowded competitive landscape?
- Your target client/customer/audience
- Your value proposition: the benefit that you will deliver that the client/customer/audience will experience
- Your pricing strategy: How will you charge for your product(s) and/or service(s) and why? How does this compare with your competitors? If your fees are less than your costs (or if you charge no fees), what is your (compelling) message to potential donors or funders?
- Your communication and/or distribution channels: How will the word get out about what you bring to the market? Why are these the best channels, given the habits and preferences of your target client/customer/audience/funder?
- Publicity: How will you publicize your work and the impact you are having to the broader community? Will you focus on press releases, news articles, electronic newsletters, special events, testimonials on your website, or social media? How will you continue to engage those that show an initial interest in your work?
- Evaluation: How will you evaluate the effectiveness of your communications?

---

15. American Marketing Association, http://www.marketingpower.com/AboutAMA/Pages/DefinitionofMarketing.aspx

If the market research you did early in the business planning process was sufficiently thorough, you should have most of the information you need to prepare a high-level plan for marketing and outreach. Be sure to consider and take advantage of the opportunity for publicity that your "launch" (however you define it) will provide.

FINANCIAL PROJECTIONS AND FUND DEVELOPMENT

Most readers of a business plan will want to jump right to the numbers. *What's the bottom line? What will this cost? Is it affordable? Are they asking for money? How much?* Well thought-out financial projections are a must for any business plan, but they present only part of the story. It is important to keep in mind that the financial projections you develop are intended to support the business plan, not the other way around. William A. Sahlman, Professor of Business Administration at Harvard Business School, had it right when he said, "As every seasoned investor knows, financial projections for a new venture are an act of imagination . . . numbers should appear mainly in the form of a business model that shows the entrepreneurial team has thought through the key drivers of the venture's success or failure."[16] Chapter 6 discusses the concept of key drivers and the steps required to create the types of financial projections necessary for most business plans. For now, suffice it to say that all the work done thus far—on strategic intent, market research and market positioning, operations and infrastructure, governance and management, the partnership model, and marketing and outreach—will inform and feed into the assumptions that form the basis of your financial projections. Those, in turn, will dictate your fund-development needs and allow you to formulate a fund-development strategy.

EVALUATION AND MEASUREMENT OF IMPACT

Evaluation is an increasingly popular topic in the nonprofit sector. Why is it so important? In short: impact. Every nonprofit seeks to have impact in the world; why else would people work so hard, often for so little remuneration? Therefore, a key question for every nonprofit is: how will we produce that impact? Doing so successfully is a continual, iterative process.

The first step is to define the desired impact. What change are you hoping to make in the world? You are working hard, to what end? Once you've done that, there is a cycle of successive actions you must take: *design programs* (that you believe will produce that impact), *measure their effectiveness* (out-

---

16.   Sahlman, William A. *How to Write a Great Business Plan*, Harvard Business School Publishing Corporation, 2008

puts, performance, progress toward outcomes, and impact), and then *evaluate* (How are we doing? How can we make our programs/activities even more effective? What changes can/should we make?). A learning orientation—an organizational and cultural commitment to inquiry and ongoing learning—is critical to success. Monitoring and evaluation provide feedback; changes to program design can be made based on that feedback.

The process just described—design, measure, evaluate, repeat—is typically applied to a nonprofit's programmatic strategies. It is equally applicable (and important) when planning for the type of major change that drives the creation of a business plan. A new program, venture, partnership, or growth strategy is a risk; no matter how well you plan, things will not turn out exactly as you expect. Continual monitoring is a must. The planning team should define milestones for implementation and include specific check-in points in the timeline. It should also be explicit about how success will be measured. A detailed evaluation plan is not necessary at this point, but articulating key principles and metrics and committing to the process can be very helpful.

The text box below lists some of the key questions that the planning team should consider.

QUESTIONS TO CONSIDER

Evaluation and Measurement of Impact

- What will "success" look like for this undertaking? Have you articulated specific short- and long-term outcomes? If not, will you? When?

- How will you monitor and evaluate the roll-out (implementation) itself? Whose feedback will you seek? When and how?

- Will a detailed evaluation plan be created as part of implementation? Who will be responsible for creating it? Implementing it?

- Do you want or need to budget for outside assistance with a formal evaluation? Some funders will insist on it.

- With whom will you share evaluation findings?

- How will you use what you learn to improve your programs, services, and operations?

RISK AND RISK MITIGATION

Launching a new program, venture, partnership, or growth strategy can be transformative for an organization, and organizational transformation brings with it inherent risks, some that can be predicted and some that cannot. By identifying and describing the potential risks, leadership demonstrates not only that it understands them but that it is committed to finding ways to manage and mitigate them as implementation proceeds. This is an important message to send to stakeholders and, in particular, to potential funders.

Every situation is different, and thus every list of risks will be different. Strategies for mitigating the identified risks will also vary. It is critical that the planning team take time to discuss and document both and, equally important, keep both in mind as it looks to implementation. The results of your earlier business model assessment can serve as a good starting point for the discussion. Did you identify any financial "red flags" or areas of increased risk? If so, have you structured your new program, venture, partnership, or growth strategy in such a way that the risk is lowered or—even better—minimized? What more could you do to address your financial challenges? Look also at your risk reserve: is it (or will it be) at an appropriate level to deal with foreseeable contingencies, including an outright flop of your new idea? What milestones will you achieve during implementation that will indicate risks have been avoided?

Non-financial risks are equally important. Demand doesn't always meet expectations; timelines can slip; key staff may leave; new government regulations can have a dramatic effect on the economics of an industry. Ignoring these risks will not serve your ultimate goal. Instead, be honest: name what could happen and describe what you will do if it does. Having a contingency plan is critical. A too rosy picture will not impress your audience and might engender doubt that you have taken the proposed undertaking seriously.

Following are sample statements from business plans created in partnership with our clients. Each identifies a particular risk and describes strategies for addressing it.

- **Inability to be sufficiently nimble and entrepreneurial.** Successful coalitions are nimble, entrepreneurial, and highly responsive to changes in the environment. This will be especially true for [*Coalition*], which is focused on achieving an ambitious agenda within a limited time span. There is a risk that the procedures mandated by the current fiscal sponsor may impede [*Coalition's*] ability to be nimble. [*Coalition*] and the fiscal sponsor must work closely together to identify and address potential roadblocks far in advance of when they might impact [*Coalition's*] work. The working relationship to date reflects an ability to achieve this goal. In addition, although we are confident at this time that the current fiscal sponsor is the right organizational "home" for the coalition, we will revisit this issue on an annual basis. The field, funding, and organizations are dynamic; if at any point [*Coalition's*] advisory board feels that [*Coalition's*] mission could more effectively be advanced within another organizational home, a change can and will be made.

- **Insufficient attention to internal communication during the transition** could impact morale, which in turn would make the integration process more challenging. By holding ourselves to the highest standards of transparency and engaging in ongoing, frequent communication with staff, volunteers, and other key stakeholders, we will ensure that we all continue to move in the same direction toward common goals. A high-level communications plan—with specific milestones included—will guide us throughout implementation.

- **Anticipated savings through joint purchasing (e.g., of hard goods, benefits, and professional services) may not materialize to the extent hoped for,** particularly in the first two years. [*Organization*] recognizes that desired savings take time to manifest, and it will need to maintain realistic expectations even as it continues to explore ways to realize savings from its new, larger scale. Milestones for achieving expected savings will be set at intervals during implementation. Inability to achieve planned financial savings will trigger a timely analysis; where necessary, corrections will be made and new, realistic expectations set.

- **If early fundraising efforts are less successful than hoped for,** it may be difficult to truly make the cultural shift required to attract more contributed revenue long term. Skepticism is high now; a strong case must be articulated and then fully supported by such resources as skilled staff, a comprehensive fund-development plan, and clear and compelling messaging. Additionally, every early success in this area needs to be shared across the organization, building confidence and satisfaction in [*Organization's*] ability to inspire allies and generate contributions. Time must be allotted for this shift to occur. Minimum goals for increased fundraising will be set at defined intervals and fund-development plans revised if these goals are not achieved. If fundraising is lower than expected, we will have to review our growth plans.

- **If roll-out is too slow . . .** This is a low-margin business. The costs are high relative to the revenue earned—especially when "exceptional customer service" and additional on-the-ground support from [*the organizational partners*] is part of the new entity's identity. To succeed, [*Organization*] must build volume. While starting slowly in the first year might be advantageous for some reasons, it will cost us. Thus, we will work toward a rapid roll-out, while keeping a very close eye on both revenues and expenses.

- **If agency growth and a national expansion strategy concern local stakeholders . . .** Its local "roots" and reputation in the ABC County community is one of [*Organization's*] great strengths. In fact, due to its organizational history, there is a strong sense of community ownership of the organization and its self-developed curricula. [*Organization*] recognizes that, by pursuing a national growth strategy, some local stakeholders may feel that the organization is somehow stepping away from its local commitments or that the unique identity of the program will be lost. Throughout this growth process, and into the future, [*Organization*] will continue to emphasize in its communications that its local work lies at its core and that this remains highly valued. It will also need to prove this through its actions, by working to ensure that national efforts do not draw appropriate attention and/or resources away from local activities. At the heart of this growth strategy lies [*Organization's*] pride in its local work, the role this has played in its ability to create successful programs, strategies and tools, and the belief that these programs are of such a quality that they deserve to be shared more broadly.

- **If potential stakeholders in a region where [*Organization*] chooses to expand are reluctant to become involved with a national organization . . .** [*Organization*] will be diligent in all future market research efforts and target expansion into high-potential areas. Even so, there may be local stakeholders that resist partnering with an "outside" organization. Management will emphasize relationship building throughout the entire expansion process, identifying and cultivating local champions, and working with stakeholders to tailor local programming to local needs.

The plans from which these statements are taken vary tremendously in intent, but, in each case, organizational leaders thought about and discussed what could happen if things didn't go as hoped and articulated at least the beginnings of a strategy to respond. In many cases, things did not go exactly as planned, and the work done in advance enabled the organization to make corrections more rapidly: learning fast and adjusting quickly is a critical advantage.

CONCLUSION

Creating a business plan takes time. It is, by nature, an iterative process—and it should also be an inclusive one. It is an opportunity to learn, think, discuss, strategize, and test with others who share your vision for the future. It is this process, as much as the product, which provides value to those responsible for making and implementing key decisions.

CASE STUDY: KNOWLEDGE FORCE – PART 7

As Sharon and the management team continued to pull together the information needed to create a financial model, Amy received an email from Thomas. "I know everyone is ready to move on and dive into the numbers," he wrote, "but Sharon has pushed us a few times to talk about risk . . . to think about what could go wrong. We've had that conversation and included some thinking in the plan, but the final plan will be stronger if we go deeper. Here's a chart I've created building on what we've discussed. Can we have the team review it and insert something like this into the final document? We can flesh out the section on financial risk further, but this sets up the question."

After some editing by email, this is what the team approved:

	Risks	Mitigations
Reputational	Expected funding may not materialize, resulting in start/stop expansion or the need to retrench before a given expansion takes hold Knowledge Force may not dedicate the resources necessary to maintain consistently high quality control throughout all sites and schools	Establish a minimum level of firm cash commitments before moving forward with expansion into any individual location Incorporate new capacity for evaluation and quality control into the expansion plan
Financial	New staff may not be able to secure school contracts quickly, resulting in high investment with low/no financial return	Put responsibility for "informational interviews" with local school districts at national office; hold on hiring staff until a minimum number of districts has expressed interest Ensure that Baltimore area employees have deep relationships in the community
Legal	Working with children brings inherent legal liabilities	Provide training and oversight in strict adherence to national Knowledge Force standards; invest in additional training capacity at the national level to ensure consistent volunteer interactions Include a clause in every contract specifying the roles of both Knowledge Force and the school district in carrying out standards; include verbal discussion of legal risks and responsibilities in a semi-annual district check-in by national staff
Program Integrity	Critical current staff may leave mid-expansion, leaving the organization with insufficient skill sets or human capacity to complete the expansion appropriately Work product of new staff may not initially meet national standards Lack of diversity among retirees may not reflect diversity of students	Create "golden handcuffs" agreement with key managers during implementation period to ensure expert oversight of new metro area Pace implementation of new programs at a level that affords close national and regional oversight, particularly in the first two years Determine whether the diversity of volunteers is a priority and develop strategies to maintain the composition desired

CHAPTER 6:

PROJECTING THE FUTURE: BUSINESS PLAN FINANCIALS

Successful business planning requires the development of an economic logic that is both sound and defensible. In this chapter, we will walk through a process for describing and analyzing your undertaking in financial terms. As we proceed, you will see that the primary goal is not to develop a perfectly accurate prediction of revenues and expenses; rather, it is to test assumptions about key economic drivers, those variables that most influence the scale and financial sustainability of an undertaking. To move forward, you should identify and consider every important financial assumption and then use the process of creating a multi-year budget as a means to demonstrate that the financial elements of the venture's success are well understood by the team spearheading the effort. As noted previously, most investors would agree that the skill, talent, and expertise of the team undertaking the venture are what matter most, not the numbers they develop. The business plan is an opportunity to demonstrate to board members and investors/funders the quality of your thinking and thus your management acumen. It is also a way to uncover any minor, major, or potentially fatal flaws in your assumptions—before it is too late.

> Economic drivers are those variables that most influence the scale and financial sustainability of an undertaking.

BUILDING FINANCIAL PROJECTIONS

Chapter 3 focused on understanding and evaluating your business model, a key aspect of which is your financial health. With that understanding as a baseline, you can now begin the process of quantifying your new program, venture, partnership, or growth strategy. This stage of the process is highly iterative and will likely involve making changes—perhaps major ones—to the concept you have developed. The future is always uncertain, and this process provides the perfect opportunity to test the viability of your model without having to deal with any real-world consequences. This concept has been described as the 1-10-100 rule: $1 spent on prevention will save $10 on correction and $100 on failure costs. The time-honored way of saying this: an ounce of prevention is worth a pound of cure.

THREE IMPORTANT FINANCIAL STATEMENTS

You should always include a multi-year budget in your business plan, along with a narrative that explains the key drivers underlying your projections and all related assumptions. We also recommend including cash flow and balance sheet projections. Although the statements themselves are important, the real value comes from the process of developing them and in the refinement to the overall concept that results.

Below is a brief description of each financial statement:

- **Multi-Year Budget**: The multi-year budget projects your revenues, expenses, and surplus/deficit over a specified time horizon. It will paint a picture of your venture and show whether or when it will break even or generate a surplus. A three-year budget (perhaps presented on a monthly or quarterly basis in the first year) is typical, keeping in mind that the further into the future you project, the less accurate the numbers tend to be. Remember that there is a difference between budget projections and cash flow projections; the revenues and expenses projected in a multi-year budget do not necessarily reflect the receipt and disbursements of cash. Many organizations (both for-profit and nonprofit) go out of business because of an inability to meet cash demands, even if long-term financial prospects as presented in a multi-year budget are good.

- **Cash Flow Projections**: Cash flow projections show the anticipated inflow and outflow of cash—by month—over a projection period, which is typically 12-24 months. Cash flow projections help you understand how much cash you will need and how much you will actually have on hand at any given time. This, in turn, will inform your estimates for capital investment, start-up funding, and/or growth-capital needs and timing.

- **Balance Sheet Projections**: The balance sheet—also known as the statement of financial position—presents a snapshot of your organization's assets (what you own), liabilities (what you owe), and net assets (the difference between the two). In the nonprofit sector, it is relatively uncommon to project a balance sheet forward; however, it can be an effective way to examine the implications of future plans, especially if they involve a merger (consolidation of assets and liabilities) or the purchase or upgrade of significant property, plant, and equipment (PP&E).

Depending on the details of your venture, preparing your projections and presenting them in the format described can be more or less time-consuming. There is always complexity, however, as the goal is to integrate multiple variables related to the undertaking, test a variety of different assumptions, and identify the financial implications of your decisions.

SEVEN STEPS TO BUILDING FINANCIAL PROJECTIONS

There are many approaches to developing financial statements for a business plan. We have found it helpful to follow the seven steps described below.

Step 1: Identify the individual(s) responsible for preparing the financial projections

It may seem obvious, but be sure not to overlook this step. The person who prepares the projections may not be the same person who presents them to the board or to investors and funders. If the members of the planning team do not have an adequate comfort level with spreadsheets or lack the necessary financial expertise, you will want to engage someone—a CFO, accountant, or consultant—who knows how to do this work. However, you must ensure that the business planning team is actively involved in each step of the development and revision of the projections, based on their exploration of assumptions and risk. The individual or team presenting the plan must fully understand the numbers and the assumptions behind them. Remember, the purpose of the financial projections is both to inform decision making by the business planning team and to demonstrate the knowledge and expertise of the leadership team.

Step 2: Identify and test overarching assumptions

No one can say with absolute certainty what will happen tomorrow, let alone in three months or three years. Those responsible for business planning must develop projections based on articulated *assumptions*. Assumptions fall into two categories: overarching and those related to specific financial drivers. Financial projections (which, taken together with the assumptions that feed into them, are often referred to as the financial model) are more than educated guesses—they are based on market research as well as experience— but they are only *indicative* of the future, not fully accurate or predictive. The planning team's assumptions are key contributors to the financial model. Therefore, the usefulness of any given set of projections will be completely dependent on the validity of the assumptions underlying the numbers used.

Overarching assumptions describe "big-picture" expectations about the financial viability of a particular venture. Other assumptions are tied to the specific variables that most influence the scale and sustainability of the initiative, the key financial drivers.

It is not difficult to imagine an organization's developing a terrific plan around a set of assumptions that don't fit with reality. Consider the following example:

An agency with a strong reputation in its local community developed several highly successful programs that support substance abuse treatment and violence prevention for urban, ethnically diverse youth ages 14-17. The programs were extensively evaluated and tested and recently received several high-profile awards. The Executive Director and board believed that now was the time to launch a new line of business: selling the organization's curricula and related merchandise to other nonprofit organizations across the nation, turning a profit for the agency that could be used to fund growth. The agency developed a detailed financial plan that articulated the up-front and ongoing costs of expansion, a pricing structure, and projected volume of sales that would make the new line of business profitable within a two-year period. The pricing structure was based on the cost for similar curricula as displayed on a prominent searchable online registry. The volume assumptions were based on attracting a relatively small percentage of would-be users in the national market. Both the senior management team and the board were quite excited to find that the financial model projected a positive outcome!

The agency hired outside consultants to test the competitive environment and the size of the market it was planning to enter. The results were sobering. After researching several competitors who were selling similar curricula on a national scale, the consultants learned that all were heavily dependent on grant funding to support their operations; other agencies selling curricula on a national scale generated enough revenue to cover only 15%-30% of the actual cost of the endeavor. This was due to several factors, including the substantial investment required simply to maintain the existing customer base (fees were difficult to renew) and a trend toward more "open-source" activity for such curricula. Further, at least one of the competitors was heavily subsidized by a foundation, enabling it to "give away" its curricula and exacerbating price competition in the field. (How do you compete with free?) Bottom line: the assumption that this venture would be profitable simply from sales of curricula and related merchandise was not realistic.

Once the agency's leaders had recovered from the initial shock and disappointment, they reconvened and looked at expansion with fresh eyes. They ultimately determined that expansion nationally was—from a mission perspective—an imperative. They then went about developing a business plan that included in its assumptions the need for fundraising from individuals, foundations, and government to support the growth.

This agency's overarching assumption was that sales of curricula and related merchandise to other nonprofits would generate a surplus that the organization could use to cover its program costs as it grew. Other assumptions— about optimal pricing and likely sales volume—seemed reasonable given the results of early online research. Fortunately, the agency didn't stop there, as additional research highlighted several shortcomings in the proposed model.

If the agency had created a chart to note and track its overarching assumptions, the first row might have looked something like Figure F.

Assumption	Evidence To Support Assumption	Additional Research Required	Strategic Questions To Be Considered
Sales of curricula and related merchandise to other nonprofits will generate a surplus that can be used to support other mission-based activities as we grow.	Pricing of similar curricula displayed on a searchable online registry.\n\nThe volume of sales required to reach profitability is a small percentage of the overall market.	Research competitors that sell curricula on a national scale to understand their business models.	Do we continue with the expansion plan if it will not be profitable?

Figure F: Overarching Assumptions

Be intentional about articulating financial assumptions as you go through the process of developing your plan. Take time to research, test, and revise your assumptions until you have enough information to rigorously defend each one in the business plan. Because you may be "too close" to the situation, colleagues, consultants, or other individuals with both knowledge and distance should review and add to your list of assumptions—and try to poke holes in them.

Identifying your assumptions is, of course, a necessary step in preparing the financial model. Describing them explicitly has another benefit as well: it can help naysayers discuss their concerns with the planning team in a helpful way. If you have assumed that you will be able to raise $100,000, for example, you could simply plug that number into the model. Or you could provide additional detail: the $100,000 was based on an assumption that 10 out of 30 potential, named donors will contribute $10,000. Rather than attacking the $100,000 figure, a board member can question the research around these potential donors, and you can demonstrate the basis for your projection.

Step 3: Identify key financial drivers

Recall that the purpose of developing financial statements for a business plan is to demonstrate a clear understanding of how the business model functions—and to identify where any weaknesses may exist so you can improve the plan and ensure a higher likelihood of success. Defining the key revenue and expense drivers—those variables that most influence the scale and sustainability of the initiative—and testing assumptions about the likely values of each will help you determine how best to refine and implement your model.

Take, for example, Knowledge Force, which (in our case study) is seeking to expand its K-3 tutoring program into new geographies. After reviewing the pricing at two of the most successful sites, the planning team projected that each new school will pay between $5,000 and $25,000 per year for the Knowledge Force program. Total revenues from participating schools, a critical component of the financial model, then depend on two drivers: the number of schools reached within a particular timeframe and the average revenue generated per school. Varying these factors will allow the planning team to see a range of possible outcomes. Table 1 presents the planning team's initial assumptions for each key financial driver, along with the associated outcomes.

Revenue Driver	Assumption								
Number of Schools	Between 10 and 20 in Year 1; growing by 15-40 each year								
Average Revenue Per School	Estimate $5K-$25K per school								
K-3 Tutoring Program	Year 1			Year 2			Year 3		
Number of Schools	10	15	20	25	30	40	40	60	80
Avg. School Revenue at $5K	$50	$75	$100	$125	$150	$200	$200	$300	$400
Avg. School Revenue at $10K	$100	$150	$200	$250	$300	$400	$400	$600	$800
Avg. School Revenue at $15K	$150	$225	$300	$375	$450	$600	$600	$900	$1,200
Avg. School Revenue at $20K	$200	$300	$400	$500	$600	$800	$800	$1,200	$1,600
Avg. School Revenue at $25K	$250	$375	$500	$625	$750	$1,000	$1,000	$1,500	$2,000

Table 1: Revenue Drivers and Projected School Revenues for New Metro Area, Years 1-3

Note: *Dollar values are in thousands*

As you prepare and review this type of analysis, be sure to refer to step two and confirm that the assumptions you have made about price (e.g., the schools' willingness and ability to pay within the stated range) and volume (both market penetration and rate of growth) have been tested and are valid. In this example, the assumptions are highly reliable because they are based on current experience. An organization expanding into a completely new program area may need to do more extensive research to identify and confirm its assumptions. Ultimately, your ability to demonstrate the validity of your assumptions—particularly to an outside audience—may make or break your endeavor.

On the expense side (and continuing to use Knowledge Force as an example), both the number of schools brought online and the projected rate of growth will impact personnel costs. Given the organization's heavy reliance on volunteers (including volunteer coordinators), the Knowledge Force planning team will need to analyze staff capacity and identify the costs related to adding both volunteers and staff as additional schools are brought online. Cost drivers would include the number of children per school and the number of children that can be served (on average) by each volunteer tutor. Knowledge Force must then determine the number of volunteers/volunteer coordinators that can be effectively managed by a single Program Manager and, thus, the number of Program Managers required. See Table 2, below, which Knowledge Force derived from its current experience. Knowledge Force also provides critical national program support, in such areas as curriculum development, staff training, and new-site development; program expansion anywhere in the system will impact its need to expand capacity in these areas. Finally, the need for administrative, fund development, and other support staff—often underestimated—must also be considered.

Cost Driver	Assumption
K-3 students per school	250
Students served per (volunteer) tutor	12
(Volunteer) tutors required per school *Note: this assumes 100% of children in each school are served	21 **(calculated)**
Number of (volunteer) tutors per (volunteer) School Coordinator Note: this assumes each school will have one tutor who serves as Team Leader, managing and coordinating the other tutors at the school Note: School Coordinators are volunteers but do receive an annual stipend to recognize their time commitment	84
Number of (volunteer) School Coordinators managed by each (paid) Program Manager	8
Number of Program Managers required per school Note: Assumes that one Program Manager can manage up to 30 schools	0.03 **(calculated)**

Table 2: Cost Drivers for Proposed Expansion

In this example, each School Coordinator can oversee tutors at up to four schools. The number of tutors and School Coordinators required will depend on the number of schools implementing the program. Table 3 presents projections for the numbers of schools shown in Table 1.

K-3 Tutoring Program	Year 1			Year 2			Year 3		
Number of Schools	10	15	20	25	30	40	40	60	80
Number of Tutors Required	210	315	420	525	630	840	840	1260	1680
Number of School Coordinators Required	3	4	5	6	8	10	10	15	20
Number of Program Managers Required	1	1	1	1	1	2	2	2	3

Table 3: Staffing Projections for Proposed Expansion

When doing this type of analysis for your own planning process, be sure to thoroughly test and reconcile the assumptions behind each driver, especially if you do not have current data to support your estimates.

Step 4: Test various scenarios

One of the most valuable tools for testing and refining the economics of an undertaking is a spreadsheet-based financial model that lets you plug in different values for each of the key assumptions and see how changes in those values will impact the bottom line. Through such a process, you can see the likely financial outcome of a range of scenarios. You can identify what the "best-case" and "worst-case" scenarios are likely to be and can plan accordingly. Think of a scenario as a set of assumptions: if there are five drivers in a proposed initiative, choosing a value for each forms one scenario; choosing a different set of values for one or more of the drivers forms another scenario. You may need to generate multiple scenarios, then narrow down to the two to three that seem most likely or that define the outer likelihood of best and worst case. For a relatively complex undertaking, you may identify five to twelve critical drivers; a simpler pursuit may require the exploration of only two to four drivers.

The set-up of the financial model will vary, but you can expect to see several common building blocks that relate to either expense drivers or revenue drivers.

The key expense driver in most cases will be the staffing structure and the assumptions underlying it. You may find it helpful to run multiple staffing scenarios—possibly categorizing them as Optimal, Base Case, and Bare Bones—to help you understand the implications of choosing one option over another. Begin by listing all current and projected staff positions, with title and (fully loaded) salary. See the example below (Table 4), which represents the staffing structure for a new Knowledge Force "site," or metropolitan area.

Staff Positions	Base	Taxes & Benefits	Fully Loaded Salary (Cost)
Senior Program Manager	$90,000	25.0%	$112,500
Program Manager	$50,000	25.0%	$62,500
Volunteer Recruiter	$50,000	25.0%	$62,500
Trainer	$45,000	25.0%	$56,250
Development Associate	$40,000	25.0%	$50,000
Program Assistant	$40,000	25.0%	$50,000

Table 4: Salary Estimates for Proposed Expansion

After settling on estimated salaries for each position, articulate assumptions for each of three staffing scenarios. (See Table 5.) It is important to discuss the assumptions underlying each scenario with members of the planning team and, often, with other staff members and/or stakeholders. Current staffers often have the most nuanced understanding of what it takes to get work done. You may learn, for example, that your "Bare Bones" scenario is completely untenable from a programmatic or operations standpoint—meaning it will need to be revised.

Year 1 Staffing Model	Optimal	Base Case	Bare Bones
Number of FTEs	6 FTEs	4 FTEs	3 FTEs
Senior Program Manager	$112,500	$112,500	$112,500
Program Manager	$62,500	$62,500	$62,500
Volunteer Recruiter	$62,500	$62,500	$62,500
Trainer	$56,250	$56,250	0
Development Associate	$50,000	0	0
Program Assistant	$50,000	0	0
Total	$393,750	$293,750	$237,500

Table 5: Three Staffing Scenarios for Proposed Expansion

Depending on the nature of your endeavor, you may also need to run scenarios for non-personnel expenses, e.g., additional office space or additional marketing costs. Projected costs can be presented in detail as shown in Table 6, or summarized (by category). Keep in mind also that any anticipated one-time (i.e., nonrecurring) costs associated with the venture will need to be included in your scenarios.

Operating Expenses	Highest	Base Case	Bare Bones
Salary and Benefits	$ 393,750	$ 293,750	$ 237,500
Consulting/Professional Fees	75,000	50,000	0
Stipends for Volunteers (coordinators and team leads)	25,000	18,750	0
Rent	41,250	32,500	28,750
Travel	14,400	14,400	14,400
Meetings	8,100	5,400	4,050
Professional Fees	6,500	6,500	6,500
Office Supplies	3,750	2,500	1,875
Printing and Publications	13,425	13,425	13,425
Telephone/Internet	6,500	6,500	6,500
Insurance	4,300	4,300	4,300
Professional Development	2,400	1,600	1,200
Postage and Delivery	1,300	1,300	1,300
Other Expenses	950	650	450
Allocation for National Service Support	211,874	185,500	141,250
Total Operating Expenses	$ 808,499	$ 637,075	$ 461,500

Table 6: Three Expense Scenarios for Proposed Expansion

Developing scenarios for revenues can be equally straightforward. In the Knowledge Force example (see Table 7 below), revenue projections are based on the following drivers and assumptions:

1. **Revenues per school:** The premise, based on current experience, is that each school will pay a fixed price to have Knowledge Force volunteers tutor children in their school. The assumption is that each school will pay between 5,000 and 25,000 for Knowledge Force's services.

2. **Number of participating schools:** This will determine the volume of sales, as each school represents a certain amount of revenue. The rate at which schools come online is also important and will be a key determinant of success or failure.

3. **Foundation and individual support:** Increases in contributed revenue are notoriously difficult to predict, and all assumptions should be thoroughly vetted and described. Where financial risk for a new endeavor is high, a prudent board may require more-detailed development plans or a minimum threshold of new financing before launch.

Year 1 Revenues	Optimal	Base Case	Bare Bones
Revenues Per School	$25,000	$15,000	$5,000
Number of Schools	20	15	10
Total School Revenues	$500,000	$225,000	$50,000
Foundation Support	$19,150	$16,170	$12,896
Individual Support	$45,400	$40,425	$12,896
Total Revenue	$564,550	$281,595	$75,792

Table 7: Three Revenue Scenarios for Proposed Expansion

Once the planning team has developed scenarios for both revenues and expenses, it is time to put them together. The first task is to look at the bottom line in the overall best-case and worst-case scenarios. To calculate a best-case bottom line, take the "optimal" total revenues less the "bare bones" total expenses; to calculate a worst-case bottom line, take the "bare bones" total revenues less the "optimal" (highest) total expenses (Table 8). Taken together, the results serve as the likely outer limits for the range of possible outcomes.

As shown in Table 8, this process reveals that the proposed new Metro Area could generate a surplus only under the very best of circumstances (optimal revenues and bare bones expenses)—and could see a catastrophic (about $730,000) deficit under a worst-case scenario. Table 9 shows three additional scenarios, each yielding a bottom line somewhere between the "best case" and "worst case."

Year 1 "Best Case"	
Optimal Revenues	$564,550
Bare Bones Expenses	$461,500
Surplus/Deficit	$103,050

Year 1 "Worst Case"	
Bare Bones Revenue	$75,792
Highest Expenses	$808,499
Surplus/Deficit	$(732,707)

Table 8: Two Revenue and Expense Scenarios for Proposed Expansion, Year 1

YEAR 1 REVENUES & EXPENSES			
	High Revenues & Expenses	Base Revenues & Expenses	Bare Bones Revenues & Expenses
Total Revenues	$564,550	$281,595	$75,792
Total Expenses	$808,499	$637,075	$461,500
Surplus/Deficit	$(243,949)	$(355,480)	$(385,708)

Table 9: Three Mid-Range Revenue and Expense Scenarios, Year 1

Tables 8 and 9 highlight the likely need for an up-front capital investment to cover initial budget deficits. This analysis does not speak to the ongoing sustainability of the venture, however. The question thus becomes, will the venture eventually break even (or generate a surplus) and, if so, when and under what scenario? For example, will a base-case revenue scenario be sufficient, or will best-case revenues be required? Expanding the financial model further out in time and incorporating increasingly refined revenue and expense estimates will bring these answers into focus.

After reviewing various scenarios, the Knowledge Force planning team found that the only way to implement a sustainable expansion would be to reach 60 schools by Year 3, with annual fees averaging $15,000 per school. Table 10 shows the financial projections on which Knowledge Force ultimately based its decisions. In this example, the major revenue driver for the proposed expansion site is school fees. Note that contributed revenues are revised down from the optimal projections, as often happens once the local fundraising environment is more fully understood. This example also assumes a final choice to move forward with the best-case staffing scenario because the base-case and the bare-bones scenario would stretch existing staff too thin.

	Year 1 Projection	Year 2 Projection	Year 3 Projection
Operating Revenues (base case)			
School Revenues	$ 225,000	$ 450,000	$ 900,000
Foundation Support	16,170	18,582	49,106
Individual Support	40,425	46,456	49,106
Total Operating Revenues	281,595	515,038	998,212
Operating Expenses (highest case)			
Salary and Benefits	393,750	467,656	479,348
Consulting/Professional Fees	75,000	75,000	50,000
Stipends for Volunteers (coordinators and team leads)	25,000	50,000	100,000
Rent	41,250	41,250	41,250
Travel	14,400	19,200	21,600
Meetings	8,100	9,450	9,450
Professional Fees	6,500	6,500	6,500
Office Supplies	3,750	4,375	4,375
Printing and Publications	13,425	13,425	13,425
Telephone/Internet	6,500	8,000	8,500
Insurance	4,300	4,300	4,300
Professional Development	2,400	2,800	2,800
Postage and Delivery	1,300	1,500	1,550
Other Expenses	950	979	1,008
Allocation for National-Service Support	211,874	224,685	238,012
Total Operating Expenses	808,499	929,119	982,117
Surplus/Deficit	$ (526,904)	$ (414,081)	$ 16,094

Table 10: Multi-year Budget for Proposed Expansion

Step 5: Prepare the financial statements

Once you have completed steps 1-4, preparing the financial statements should be fairly straightforward, although you may go through multiple iterations as you continue to test and revise different assumptions. As you do so, be sure to take into account historical trends and your organization's past financial performance. If there are major inconsistencies between past performance and future projections, be very clear about what assumptions were used and why you chose those. What do you think will change in the future and why?

Multi-Year Budget

The multi-year budget is the obvious place to begin. Depending on whether this is a new venture with many unknowns or an expansion of an existing program, you may want to begin with monthly projections or look first to a quarterly or annual presentation. When building your projections, we recommend that you first insert your expenses, beginning with staffing and then moving to non-personnel costs. Identify all recurring costs, then consider and add in any non-recurring (one-time) costs. These might include legal and/or consulting fees, expenses related to setting up an office in a new city, initial investment in equipment, or a special marketing campaign tied to the launch of the new program. Next, drop in your projected earned revenues.[17] Finally, project your contributed revenue from such sources as individuals, foundations, or corporations that will support the program on an ongoing basis.

Table 11 shows the multi-year budget summary for the entire Knowledge Force agency, inclusive of both existing program revenues and expenses and the new Metro Area expansion described above. As a general rule, presentation of the multi-year budget, like all financial statements, should be as simple and clear as possible while being responsive to the needs of the intended audience.

	Year 1 Projection	Year 2 Projection	Year 3 Projection
Operating Revenues			
National Office and Current Program Revenue	$2,987,883	$3,062,580	$3,139,145
New Fundraising by National Office	75,000	100,000	300,000
One-Time Growth Capital (Uncommitted)[18]	425,000	550,000	
One-Time Growth Capital (Committed)[19]	250,000	50,000	—
New Metro Area Expansion	281,595	515,038	998,212
Total Revenues	4,019,478	4,277,618	4,437,356
Operating Expenses			
National Office	1,002,241	1,027,297	1,052,979
National Incremental Expansion Costs	410,250	470,600	533,766
Current Metro Area Programs	1,985,642	2,035,283	2,086,165
New Metro Area Expansion	808,499	929,119	982,117
Total Expenses	4,206,632	4,462,299	4,655,027
Operating Surplus/Deficit	(187,154)	(184,681)	(217,671)
Costs Allocable to New Metro Area	211,874	224,685	238,012
Operating Surplus/Deficit Post Allocation	$ 24,720	$ 40,004	$ 20,341

Table 11: Multi-year Budget for Knowledge Force

17. Earned revenues are those collected from an individual or a third party in full or partial payment for a service rendered.
18. These funds do not include a pledge from several major textbook publishers.
19. Board-designated commitment of a one-time bequest to be received over two years

A WORD ON FUNDRAISING

Beware the tendency to "plug" deficits with ever higher fundraising goals. A solid business planning process will involve anchor funders in early conversations and will rigorously test all fundraising assumptions. Based on the results of the business planning process, you may discover you need to invest more in your fundraising infrastructure to support the ongoing revenue needs of the venture. Remember that where you get the money from is driven largely by what you need the money for. You need a compelling mission-driven case, proof that qualified leadership is in place, an explanation of financial assumptions to show the venture can be sustainable, and identified supporters. The business plan ties these elements together. Most nonprofits are already doing what they can to maximize fund development; so what will change if your fundraising goal increases? For example:

- Have board members committed to expanded support and shown the capacity to carry through?
- Have major institutional donors indicated an interest in expanding their annual contribution to support the new venture?
- Are you expanding—either programmatically or geographically—in ways that will "fit" with the priorities of foundations that have not supported you in the past?
- Are you hiring new staff to better cultivate major donors or to implement a well-defined expansion of your fundraising activities?
- Has a government funder indicated a new or increased focus on the work you are doing?

If none of the above conditions pertain, resist the urge to simply enter a fundraising number that makes your projections work out. This is done all too often, usually with negative consequences.

Cash Flow Projections

If you are working within an established organization, you are probably well-versed in the process of preparing cash flow projections. The goal is to show the amount and timing of "revenue in" and "expenses out," given what you know now. For nonprofits, the timing of revenue in from foundation grants, government contracts, and well-established annual appeals or events is often fairly predictable. Likewise, many outflows are either predictable (e.g., monthly personnel costs) or can be timed through good planning (e.g., significant one-time expenses). The process of preparing cash flow projections for a new venture can highlight potential cash challenges and provide an opportunity to plan accordingly, for example by revising the date for hiring new staff or setting specific financial benchmarks prior to launch. That said, cash flow projections tend to be most accurate for the coming quarter and increasingly speculative with every month the further out you go.

In its simplest form, a cash flow statement is created through a four-step process:

1. Show the beginning cash balance on a specified date
2. Add expected cash inflows during the month
3. Subtract expected cash outflows during the month
4. Show the ending cash balance and carry it over as the beginning cash balance for the following month

A summary six-month cash flow projection from the Knowledge Force business plan is shown in Table 12; more detailed projections for Years 1-3 are shown in Table 13.

	Month 1 Projection	Month 2 Projection	Month 3 Projection	Month 4 Projection	Month 5 Projection	Month 6 Projection
Beginning Cash	$606,250	$849,449	$707,749	$608,927	$559,957	$533,319
Total Receipts	$558,411	$209,411	$224,400	$275,040	$300,454	$355,480
Total Disbursements	$315,212	$351,111	$323,222	$324,010	$327,092	$326,624
Net Cash for Period	$243,199	$(141,700)	$(98,822)	$(48,970)	$(26,638)	$28,856
Ending Cash	$849,449	$707,749	$608,927	$559,957	$533,319	$562,175

Table 12: Knowledge Force Cash Flow Projections (Summary), Months 1-6

STATEMENT OF CASH FLOWS (PROJECTED)	Year 1 Projection	Year 2 Projection	Year 3 Projection
From Operating Activity			
Surplus/Deficit from Multi-year Budget	$ 24,720	$ 40,004	$ 20,341
Depreciation (non-cash expense)	29,686	34,111	37,852
Change in Receivables	(122,471)	(100,041)	(2,503)
Change in Payables	25,542	50,012	(5,221)
Net Cash Provided by Operating Activity	(42,523)	24,086	50,469
From Investing Activity			
Purchases of Equipment	(45,000)	(20,000)	(45,000)
Net Cash Used in Investing Activities	(45,000)	(20,000)	(45,000)
Net Increase/Decrease in Cash	(87,523)	4,086	5,469
Cash Beginning of Period	606,250	518,727	522,813
Cash End of Period	$ 518,727	$ 522,813	$ 528,281

Table 13: Knowledge Force Cash Flow Projections, Years 1-3

Preparing cash flow projections will help you to identify and quantify the need for and timing of start-up capital or financing, such as a line of credit from a bank. Remember that debt, if used at all, should be used to assist with the management of cash flow rather than to cover operating shortfalls.[20] When launching a new endeavor or expanded program, taking on debt can be risky. Debt may be an appropriate tool to use for launch-related shortfalls if long-term prospects are positive. But use of debt for such purposes must be accompanied by articulation of specific financial milestones that, if met, will indicate that projections for financial sustainability are on track. An organization should always have a backup plan in mind in case those milestones are not met.

Balance Sheet
The purpose of the balance sheet is to show the financial condition of your organization at a particular point in time. Regardless of whether your focus is a start-up or an existing organization, projecting your balance sheet is a useful exercise, as is discussing with the planning team what the balance sheet should look like in two to three years' time.

20. For nonprofits with a strong balance sheet, use of short-term debt to manage normal cash flow shortfalls can be perfectly acceptable. For example, human service agencies that earn the majority of their revenue through government contracts may know that reimbursement of expenses is often delayed by up to three months at the beginning of each budget year, necessitating access to short-term debt.

Projecting a balance sheet is easier than you may think. Begin by establishing your "base period" balance sheet, the timing of which will align with the launch of your venture. (Table 14 shows the base period balance sheet for Knowledge Force.) Then incorporate the surplus or deficit from the projections in your multi-year budget (to adjust for the change in value of net assets on the balance sheet), any non-cash expenses (such as depreciation), and the information from your cash flow projections (to adjust for changes in cash, receivables, payables, capital expenditures, etc.). The projected balance sheet for Knowledge Force for years 1-3 is shown in Table 15.

STATEMENT OF FINANCIAL POSITION (BALANCE SHEET) AT FISCAL YEAR END	
Assets	
Cash	$ 606,250
Receivables	275,261
Equipment, Net	126,324
Total Assets	$ 1,007,835
Liabilities and Net Assets	
Payables and Accrued Expenses	$ 176,471
Total Liabilities	176,471
Net Assets	831,364
Total Net Assets	831,364
Total Liabilities and Net Assets	$ 1,007,835

Table 14: Knowledge Force
Base Period Balance Sheet

Balance sheet projections will enable you to track over time key metrics, such as your Current Ratio (current assets/current liabilities) and Months of Cash (cash/average monthly expenses), both important measures of liquidity. Generally speaking, it is acceptable for nonprofits to maintain a Current Ratio of at least 2 and Months of Cash of at least one and ideally three to six. You may wish to track additional balance sheet metrics, especially if your plans involve a merger or the purchase or upgrade of significant property, plant, and equipment.

	FYE Current	Year 1 Projection	Year 2 Projection	Year 3 Projection
Liquidity Metrics				
Months of Cash	2.43	1.56	1.48	1.44
Current Ratio	5.00	4.54	4.05	4.17
Assets				
Cash	$ 606,250	$ 518,727	$ 522,813	$ 528,281
Receivables	275,261	397,732	497,773	500,276
Equipment, Net	126,324	141,638	127,527	134,675
Total Assets	$ 1,007,835	$ 1,058,097	$ 1,148,113	$ 1,163,232
Liabilities and Net Assets				
Payables and Accrued Expenses	$ 176,471	$ 202,013	$ 252,025	$ 246,804
Total Liabilities	176,471	202,013	252,025	246,804
Total Net Assets	831,364	856,084	896,088	916,428
Total Liabilities and Net Assets	$ 1,007,835	$1,058,097	$ 1,148,113	$ 1,163,232

Table 15: Knowledge Force
Balance Sheet Projections, Years 1-3

In keeping with the "simple and clear" rule, you may opt not to project the entire balance sheet; however, at the very least, you should prepare to track and monitor key balance sheet data, such as the liquidity metrics shown above.

Step 6: Quantify the need for start-up capital

Any new program, venture, partnership, or growth strategy will require start-up funding or "seed capital."[21] Without it, the average nonprofit will find itself facing a deficit and perhaps a cash flow or existential crisis. (We have seen organizations that have built up reserves sufficient to cover the costs of launching a major new venture, but it is rare.) If you think your venture is the exception and will be financially self-sufficient in the first year or even during the first two or three years, think again. You may be right, but you should set a very high bar for evidence to persuade yourself, your board, and prospective investors and funders. The cost of being wrong could be financial ruin.

In the business world, the concept of seed capital is well-understood and universally accepted. In the nonprofit world, seed capital can be harder to come by. The notion of raising money for a venture that has yet to be launched can at times run counter to the more commonly applied *Field of Dreams* or "build it and the money will come" approach, which probably means that the new venture will rely wholly on the sweat equity of the management team for

21. http://www.investopedia.com/terms/s/startup-capital.asp#axzz1V9O346Cc

the foreseeable future. Clara Miller in her 2008 *Stanford Social Innovation Review* article "The Equity Capital Gap" puts it this way:

> [Start-up] equity capital plays the same role in the nonprofit and for-profit worlds: to focus a group of committed investors around a common goal. That focus gives rise to creating and maintaining a lasting enterprise that will attract both reliable buyers (such as annual givers, government contracts, tuition, or fees) and, eventually, additional equity holders. Some of the latter will be investors who periodically provide growth capital to do more.[22]

Your business plan will almost certainly require a certain amount of startup capital to succeed. The approximate amount will become evident as you test various scenarios and develop your financial projections. Keep in mind that your projections should show the point at which your venture no longer requires start-up capital. If three years is not sufficient time to reach this point of sustainability, then your plan should extend further. Keep in mind, however, that prolonged dependence on start-up capital can be risky.[23]

In the Knowledge Force example, the planning team determined that the organization would need approximately $1.275 million in growth capital to fund deficits in the first two years; by year three, both the proposed expansion site and the agency as a whole would be self-sufficient. Growth capital requirements were determined as follows:

	Year 1	Year 2	Year 3
National Incremental Expansion Costs, net of new fundraising	$335,250	$370,600	—
Metro Area Expansion Shortfalls, less allocable costs	$315,030	$189,396	—
Capital Expenditures	$45,000	$20,000	—
Total Growth Capital Required	$695,280	$579,996	—

Step 7: Consider the needs of your audience
Final preparation of your financial statements should take into account the intended audiences for your business plan and their specific needs. You want to be both thorough and clear, but it is rarely necessary to include every detail

22. Miller, Clara. "The Equity Capital Gap" in *Stanford Social Innovation Review*, Summer 2008
23. http://nonprofitfinancefund.org/files/docs/2010/BuildingIsNotBuying.pdf

or dozens of reports in the final document. A banker or PRI lender[24] may be looking for financial details that would not typically be required by a major donor or a foundation considering a grant. A board of directors may include some individuals who want to see a great deal of detail, while others want only to understand assumptions that feed into the bottom line along with any major risk factors.

Remember, before any of the audiences described above become involved in reviewing your plan, you—the team developing the plan—are its first audience. You must develop sufficiently detailed projections to satisfy your own need for information, and they must be communicated in a way that even a non-finance expert on the planning team can understand.

SEVEN DOS AND DON'TS

1. **DO** resist the urge to dive into too much detail, especially in the final plan. Keep it simple and clear. Remember that the audience is looking for the clarity of your understanding of the model. You need the detail, your audience may not.

2. **DO NOT** simply plug deficits with "to be raised" dollars. Consider and evaluate potential funding options, and the risks associated with each. Be honest about planned or potential shortfalls.

3. **DO** make sure the numbers add up. Remember, the reader will be assessing your business acumen, which includes the ability to calculate accurately (and proofread a spreadsheet).

4. **DO NOT** overwhelm the reader with too many scenarios. If you are planning to include multiple scenarios in your final plan, limit it to no more than three.

5. **DO NOT** use the word *conservative.* Any savvy investor will tell you that most new ventures do not meet their projections.

6. **DO** make sure the person or team presenting the plan to potential investors/funders understands the financial model.

7. **DO** assume that start-up capital will be a part of your business plan—and quantify the amount and timing of the need.

---

24. A PRI, or program-related investment, is a loan or other investment (as distinguished from a grant) made by a foundation to another organization for a project related to the foundation's philanthropic purposes and interests. Typically, they require repayment, but the terms involve a very low (or no) interest charge.

CONCLUSION

Financial projections are vital tools for driving internal decisions as well as communicating to an external reader that the principals understand the economic logic underlying the business plan. Remember that the purpose of financial projections is to support the business plan, not the other way around. Most important, keep in mind that the plan, including the financial analysis, is a living, breathing document and projections should be updated regularly. Identifying and testing your assumptions—financial and otherwise—should be hardwired into every step of the business planning process and extended into the implementation phase.

CASE STUDY: KNOWLEDGE FORCE – PART 8

The time had finally come for the planning team to make decisions. What recommendations did they have after all of the market research, capacity evaluation, and financial modeling?

"Remember, we start this conversation with the criteria we established in the beginning," said Sharon. "Then we add in the information we've reviewed. It's like a mathematical formula: decision-making criteria + information = strategic decision."

After reviewing all of the work done to date, the team quickly agreed that the decision came down to expanding in metropolitan Detroit, a city the organization already served, or moving into Baltimore, a new region for Knowledge Force.

Thomas summed up their thinking neatly: "These are the two areas with both great need and a high number of retirees, and the programs currently available are either not well-known locally or have not been shown to be as effective as Knowledge Force. It just makes sense."

"That's true," said Henry, "But there's still the financial analysis. I just don't see how we can afford to expand into a new city. And I'm really concerned about our capacity here in the national office; we can barely support our current programs with the staff that we have. We would need to grow centrally to support expansion into either of these areas."

"Let's look first at our financial assumptions for a new site," said Sharon. "The numbers Deborah has built out thus far are based on your current staffing and include just two positions, a Program Manager and Program Assistant. That means you could move into a new metro area with just a small capital investment: it comes to between $100,000 and $200,000 for a year or two with minimal revenue.

"With this model, you're reaching about 2,000 students annually in each metro area," she continued. "So, if you expanded to one new city per year for five years—which would be very ambitious—you'd be adding ten new staff and serving 10,000 more students. That's not even as many students as you already serve. It's growth, perhaps prudent growth, but maybe we should take some time to see what you could do with more capital."

"Right!" said Henry. "If we had additional resources to invest in growth, we could invest some of it here in DC to make sure we're bolstering our competitive advantage, investing in adequate evaluation, making curriculum changes, and—what keeps me awake at night—ensuring that our training program is state-of-the-art so that we know every volunteer is really performing at peak."

The planning team agreed to explore this further, and Sharon and Deborah walked the group through a path of inquiry.

"Here's what Deborah has prepared to show costs for a typical metropolitan office," Sharon said while Deborah projected this spreadsheet on the wall:

CURRENT SITE STAFFING	Base	Taxes & Benefits	Fully Loaded Salary (cost)
Program Manager	$50,000	25.0%	$62,500
Program Assistant	$40,000	25.0%	$50,000
Occupancy Costs			$9,000
Expenses			$10,000
Estimated Metro Location Cost			$131,500

"Now," Sharon suggested, "let's think about what you would need for this one site to go to 15,000 students over three years, doubling the size of your current program, all in one location."

"I'm not sure I like that," Deborah said. "That's the kind of aggressive expansion that we tried before Amy got here, and it nearly wiped us out."

"Right," said Sharon, "because you hadn't looked closely enough at your capital-investment needs—or made sure you could build a sustainable program in each new area once established. You may *not* have the capital, and this level of service may not be sustainable, but let's look at the numbers before we jump to that conclusion. So, what kind of staffing would you need to double in size in three years out of *one* new location?"

Sure enough, that set Henry and Amy in motion as they walked through each piece of the program. They began to talk about how the organization's under-investment in individual metropolitan areas may have held them back. By staffing each with just two people, Knowledge Force had created a natural limit on the number of students they could reach in the region. Once the Program Manager had established relationships with one or two districts; launched the program in six to twelve schools; recruited, trained, and managed 100-300 volunteers; and written three or four grant requests annually, there was naturally no time left to do anything more. Although growth *seemed* to be limited by staff size, they acknowledged that, even with unlimited staff, growth would eventually be limited by such external factors as the number of schools in a region serving low-income students and the number of volunteers available to be recruited and trained. They also acknowledged that what had held them back in existing regions was nothing more than lack of resources: they needed more staff in either the national or metro office capable of cultivating relationships with new schools and managing the resulting contracts. What Knowledge Force lacked was the ability to invest in staff focused on long-term growth rather than just immediate revenue generation. Realistically, the organization *could* grow in any high-potential region, new or existing, so long as capital was available for investment.

By posing the question of rapid growth in one region, Sharon had helped them to see the organization's potential in a new way, and they quickly began to identify what it would take to expand more rapidly.

After a 20-minute discussion, the team had compiled a list of positions necessary for a more robust metropolitan office. On the spot, Sharon and Deborah created a spreadsheet that captured a rapid-growth model:

RAPID GROWTH IN SINGLE METROPOLITAN AREA	Base	Taxes & Benefits	Fully Loaded Salary (cost)
Senior Program Manager	$90,000	25.0%	$112,500
Program Manager 1	$50,000	25.0%	$62,500
Program Manager 2	$50,000	25.0%	$62,500
Volunteer Recruiter	$40,000	25.0%	$50,000
Trainer	$40,000	25.0%	$50,000
Development Associate	$40,000	25.0%	$50,000
Program Assistant	$40,000	25.0%	$50,000

"This is great," Deborah said. "It's really not that much money, and it doesn't reflect revenues from schools or fundraising. But it also looks incomplete. We have all agreed that we need an expert in evaluation on staff and also a top-notch trainer. And then I think about my workload if we doubled in size: that would mean more data management for grants, more financial tracking, and all the rest."

"Exactly," said Sharon. "Henry and I have already done some work to model what expansion of your national capacity might look like as Knowledge Force grows. Right now, you support a barely adequate level of national services—like curriculum development and evaluation—through national fundraising. But really, you should start to look at what proportion of those services should be covered by revenues from each individual metropolitan office. You can use this process to think about the national services you really need and how much of that expense should be allocated to each regional office."

The team spent the next 30 minutes reviewing recent suggestions for how expansion of national staffing capacity could both support growth and also improve program quality. All agreed with Henry's argument that it was critical to increase the organization's capacity for training (staff and volunteer) and for partnering with academic evaluators in order to maintain the organization's competitive advantage. Deborah made a persuasive case for adding capacity around data management and information technology, while Amy insisted it was critical to continue the recent expansion in fund-development capacity; the development team would need to support an organization twice the current size *and* help raise capital for future growth.

"What about the issue of outreach and cultivating new school districts?" Sharon asked. "How can you employ capacity in that area? Is that a 'local' responsibility or a national one?" After some conversation, the group agreed that an approach similar to that used by Henry at the program level would apply here as well: Knowledge Force would add a high-visibility national Marketing Director, who could open doors to new districts and partner with Program Managers to cultivate relationships and develop new contracts.

Before long Deborah and Sharon had created a new spreadsheet, this one summarizing the additional staff capacity needed at the national level to support a dramatically bigger organization.

NEW NATIONAL STAFF POSITIONS	Base Salary	Taxes & Benefits	Fully Loaded Salary (cost)
Development Associate	$40,000	25.0%	$50,000
Director of Major Gifts	$110,000	25.0%	$137,500
Director of Information Technology	$100,000	25.0%	$125,000
Administrative Assistant 2	$40,000	25.0%	$50,000
Program Assistant	$40,000	25.0%	$50,000
Director of Learning	$110,000	25.0%	$137,500
Marketing Director	$110,000	25.0%	$137,500

The meeting had run long and had covered a great deal of ground. The group decided to call it quits and schedule a follow-up session in a couple of weeks. Before coming together again, Henry agreed to research in more detail the number of schools serving a large proportion of low-income students in the two metropolitan areas they were focused on; he needed to confirm that there really were 60 or 90 or 120 schools that Knowledge Force would want to work with within each region. Likewise, he was going to go back to some of his staff and longstanding volunteers to consider the feasibility of recruiting the hundreds, if not thousands, of volunteers that would be needed to expand in one region. Deborah was tasked with confirming the financial assumptions and working through with Henry and Amy one more time the positions needed to engage in a significant expansion.

Although Thomas and Sofia had participated in this discussion, neither had had much to say. Thomas, in particular, had been uncharacteristically quiet. Much of the conversation had been about building out staffing, which was not really his strong suit. Also, he couldn't help thinking that the exercise was interesting but not practical.

"This is really exciting," he said as the meeting was coming to a close, "but the idea of finding over a million dollars to invest, even if the numbers show it will be self-sustaining in three years, is really daunting. We've never attracted this kind of funding before, and I don't see the Gates Foundation knocking on our door. Is it even possible to find so much capital to grow this fast?"

"That is a sobering question," Sharon said. "Even if we can't pursue a full doubling in size, let's develop these numbers further so that we know what we're really talking about. We can start by analyzing this major expansion, and, in fleshing that out, we will have all the building blocks to work out the money needed for a lesser expansion."

• • •

A week and a half later, the group gathered again. Henry had confirmed the program numbers and, while admitting to some concerns about the feasibility of scaling volunteer recruitment and training to the extent that would be necessary, confirmed that, with additional human resources, it should be possible.

Thomas summed up: "What we see here is that an ambitious expansion is possible but will require more regional staff than we've considered in the past, along with new national staff to support the effort. I'm really surprised that the numbers show the work can be self-sustaining in just a few years. We will need to supplement the revenue from schools with direct contributions but only in an amount I think we can really achieve — and the risk can be kept low if we monitor actual results closely. This sustainability piece is really heartening and leaves just two big questions: can we find $1.275 million to launch this as described, or, if we find less money and need to scale it back, where do we focus expansion? Even though we've added new fundraising capacity, we project raising only a couple hundred thousand dollars over the next two years in new revenue, and I wouldn't want to commit to spending that money on something new until we see it starting to land in our bank account."

"Thanks for that," Deborah said, looking at Thomas. "All week, as I reviewed these numbers, I couldn't get the last expansion effort out of my head. We're doing great work where we are, and we almost lost all of that last time. I can't go through it again."

"We won't have to," Amy stated definitively.

"You sound pretty certain!" said Thomas. "I'm not sure if you mean that in a good way or a bad way."

Amy looked over at Sofia, who returned her knowing smile. "Can we tell them now, Sofia?" Thomas looked quizzically at Amy. "What have you two been up to?"

"Well, I think we have an option for capital investment," said Sofia. "While everyone here was digging into the numbers last week, I was in Chicago at the annual convention of School Text Publishers. I've been going to the dreaded thing for so many years, I know everyone there and decided to have fun this year. You know, I've always liked Knowledge Force, though being on the board has been a chore sometimes. But being on this committee has turned me into an evangelist. Not only was I inspired by the importance of the work—I always have been—but I got to see in a new way the quality of Amy's leadership and the way Henry and Deborah dig into things. I knew that, with this great team in charge, it was time to get off my butt and extract a little good out of those bigwigs at the conference.

"I kept thinking about the preliminary budget numbers discussed at our last meeting and realized that I had the information I needed to start this thing moving. Before I left for the conference, I set up a meeting with Amy and my CEO, who just happens to be a native of Maryland. Although he has known about our contribution to Knowledge Force, it has never really been high on his radar, and I figured it was time to change that. Amy came in with two pieces of paper. The first included nothing more than eight bullet points, each describing in one sentence a study that showed how Knowledge Force's results exceeded those of any other tutoring program. The second sheet of paper had nothing except the statement '$1,000,000 over two years means 30% of Maryland's lowest-income K-3 students will learn to read.'"

You could just about hear the jaws hitting the floor.

"You didn't!" said Henry.

"I sure did," said Amy, unable to contain her laughter. "We've got something great to sell, and we've shown what it would take to make it work. Because of what we've done here, I had everything I needed on the tip of my tongue."

"So my boss, he just looked at Amy," Sofia continued. "Then he said, 'Well, we better do something about this.' Within the next half hour, he'd agreed to work with me to create a challenge grant to the other three major textbook publishers. He pledged to match 25¢ for each 25¢ pledged by the other publishers, up to $100,000 per year for two years.

"Amy and I spent three days creating a pitch for the other companies," she added. "I can't believe how much fun I had at the convention! My boss and I found each CEO and, one by one, handed them the packets. He cajoled each CEO to commit right on the spot! We got every single one: $800,000 total!"

"I've spent the last week biting my tongue," Amy said. "Sofia made me swear not to say anything until today. I know I was being a nudge, Deborah, when I kept asking you to confirm our numbers after the last meeting; I needed them sooner than you knew, and I had to know they were right. What Thomas said is what we confirmed over the past week: that the expansion is feasible and, over time, will be self-sustaining but we just didn't have the capital. Even before Sofia came up with this idea, I knew that our decision would come down to start-up funds. Then, Sofia told me what she was thinking, and when I Googled her boss and saw that he was a Maryland native, I knew what we had to do. We can base our operations in the city of Baltimore. If we can saturate the school district there and in nearby low-income areas, we'll have reached a major portion of the children in need in the state."

"So how much money are we talking about again?" asked Thomas.

"Well, it's several shekels short of a full pot of gold," said Sofia. "The one catch—and I think it's a good one—is that Knowledge Force will have to provide an equal match to each of the publishers, or $200,000."

"It doesn't matter how Knowledge Force finds it." Amy jumped in, "We'll have to sell the plan to some other foundations or major donors or try to jump-start our fund-development expansion. We'll have to find it somewhere. I've already started work with Olivia and the Development staff to identify exactly whom we can approach and for how much. This is a great opportunity and a solid plan. I really think it's salable, especially with the textbook match in hand."

"We'll have to word the board's approval to include that," Thomas said, "But this is now the easiest decision I've ever made. I'm ready to move that we recommend proceeding with an expansion into the Baltimore metropolitan area without delay!"

"I understand your enthusiasm," laughed Sharon, "but I'm sorry to say that you have a business plan to wrap up first."

Needless to say, no one in that room ever lacked appreciation for Sofia again.

CHAPTER 7
PULLING IT ALL TOGETHER

Congratulations! At this point in the business planning process, the bulk of your work is done. You have clarified strategic intent; done market research and defined your market position; designed and described an infrastructure to support your venture; decided how and by whom it will be led; defined the nature and structure of key collaborative relationships; prepared comprehensive financial projections and *pro forma* financial statements; decided how you will monitor, measure, and evaluate progress and impact; and identified both risks and strategies for their mitigation. It is now time to pull all of your work together into a final document: the business plan. This is the formalization of the last phase in the *DARE² Succeed* framework, elaborating on the chosen model.

THE EXECUTIVE SUMMARY

At the risk of stating the obvious, a good business plan always begins with an Executive Summary. Many, if not most, of your readers will not have the inclination or patience to read every page in detail. Therefore, it is critical that you make your case clearly and persuasively right up front. Describe what you are proposing and why that program, venture, partnership, or growth strategy is compelling. Explain—at the highest level only—what market or customer need you are meeting and how the undertaking will fit into the competitive landscape. Name the leader or, better still, the leadership team to instill in your readers the confidence that the leadership can execute successfully. Summarize the financial realities. For example: with X of initial investment, your program, venture, partnership, or growth strategy will launch over the course of Y months and generate Z in revenues over the next three years, at which point you expect fees and ongoing fundraising to cover all ongoing costs. If the audience for your plan is a potential funder or investor, be clear on what you are asking for and about why the investment is a good one. The business plan is about the business of advancing your mission.

Note that, although the Executive Summary is the first section of the plan, it is typically written at the end of the process, once everything else is complete. You can't summarize what you haven't written, after all! As a rule of thumb, discipline yourself to a maximum of two pages for the Executive Summary.

MISSION, VISION, AND DESIRED IMPACT

After the Executive Summary comes the crux of your case statement: a description of your mission, vision, and desired impact. You have a compelling idea; you want the reader to see it, understand it, and be inspired by it! Think of the case statement as all the best reasons to undertake the initiative you propose. Use it to overcome any obvious objections. As with the Executive Summary, try to keep this to less than two pages. Often one page is sufficient.

THE PROGRAM, ORGANIZATION, OR INITIATIVE

This is the "what," a description of exactly what you are proposing. Here are a few examples of how such a description might start.

- *Fabulous Families is an evidence-based family education program designed to enhance communication between parents and children, strengthen the family bond, and support school success by targeting three key areas: parenting skills, intrafamily communication, and the home/school partnership. Each element of the program builds on our organization's existing core competencies while extending our reach— and thus our impact—in new ways.*

- *The Children's Performing Arts Collaborative, a joint venture among the six most prominent performing arts organizations in the Metro Area, will provide an opportunity for youth throughout the region to learn about, participate in, and view live performances from a wide variety of disciplines and styles. Children between the ages of 6 and 18 will be exposed to performance art in school and through low-cost after-school programs. Instruction will focus on live performance as well as backstage skills, including set design, costume design, lighting, and sound.*

- *Animals for All, a national nonprofit dedicated to the idea that every individual deserves to experience the human-animal bond through a caring relationship with a pet, currently advances its mission through the work of a parent organization and 12 affiliates. Over the past 25 years, through our individual and collective efforts, we have made great strides in advancing our mission. Now, however, the time is right to unify, to bring our 13 corporate entities into one and, in doing so, to dramatically increase our ability to launch national initiatives for greater impact, take advantage of economies of scale, and enhance our program and brand awareness.*

More detail would follow, of course, but your description need not be exhaustive; anything over a page is probably too long. The point is to be crystal clear about who you are (as an organization or group of organizations working together) and what you are proposing to do.

THE MARKET

In this section, summarize what you learned through your market research. Provide a "big-picture" description of what's happening in your market. Describe the need for your product, service, or organization and specify the population(s) you are seeking to attract and/or serve. Identify other key players in that space (including your top competitors) and be clear on your competitive advantage. This section should be one to three pages long.

MANAGEMENT AND OPERATIONS

Here is where you wow your audience with a description of your leadership team's qualifications. Depending on the size and scope of what you are proposing, this may include a description of your board and a list of board members; brief bios of the CEO and other key staff leaders; and/or a description of any planned search processes. Include your organizational chart, accompanied by a brief explanation. (A picture may be worth a thousand words, but that doesn't necessarily mean an unfamiliar reader will be able to home in on the most important elements of your chart.)

There is no "right length" for the overview of operations and infrastructure. We've seen some great plans for relatively contained initiatives that covered the operational highlights in just a few short pages. We've also seen plans that—due both to the complexity of the proposed entity and to the needs of a specific audience (e.g., board members asked to approve a significant investment in a major change process, staff planning to use the plan to guide implementation)—went into great detail in each functional area. Each planning team must decide for itself what level of detail is necessary and what will best serve the undertaking.

KEY COLLABORATIVE RELATIONSHIPS/PARTNERSHIP MODEL (IF A PARTNERSHIP)

Not all business plans focus on an undertaking that involves organizational partners. If yours does, briefly describe the partners and partnership model in your plan. Include a description of how each partner will be involved in oversight and a description of how staffing will be shared (or not). If there will be specific legal documents governing the partnership (e.g., an MOU or merger agreement), describe these.

If the focus of your plan is *not* a formal partnership but success will depend at least in part on certain key collaborative relationships, describe these.

MARKETING AND OUTREACH

This section builds on the information presented earlier in the plan, in the section on the Market. If you were clear about the population(s) you seek to attract and/or serve and the competitive advantage that will lead them to your organization (rather than to a competitor), describe how you will make your target demographic aware of what you bring to the market. Include specifics about message content, communication channels, and value proposition. Describe how you will reach out to—and maintain the interest of—new audiences, as well as existing clientele who may not be aware of all that you offer. Include a description of your social-media strategy, along with an acknowledgement that it may change as norms in the sector change.

FINANCIAL PROJECTIONS AND FUND DEVELOPMENT

Chapter 6 outlined a process for preparing financial projections that includes conversation, spreadsheet modeling, and iterative refinements leading to a "final" (for purposes of the business plan) set of projections. These are typically shown via a *pro forma* Multi-year Budget, Cash Flow Projections, and Balance Sheet. The statements themselves are best included in an Appendix, with the "bottom line" shown in the body of the plan. Accompanying that summary should be a description of the assumptions on which the projections were built and how those assumptions were tested, along with descriptions of anticipated start-up costs and capital requirements. Remember that some readers love numbers, while others prefer a narrative presentation of the financial picture. Provide both. If the focus of the business plan is a partnership, include a description of how costs and (if applicable) revenues will be shared. Finally, describe your plans for securing revenue for the initiative through fund development and, if applicable, earned income; how will costs be covered, both in the short term and long term?

EVALUATION AND MEASUREMENT OF IMPACT

While it is true that a business plan rarely needs a comprehensive evaluation plan, it should include a brief statement about the importance of monitoring, evaluation, and measurement of impact and an overview of the mechanisms that will be put in place to ensure that all three occur. An implementation timeline should be included describing milestones, metrics, decision points, and other decision-making criteria.

RISK AND RISK MITIGATION

Typically brief but incredibly important, this section summarizes the potential risks facing the organization and its leadership team as it moves forward with implementation, along with a statement of how each risk will be monitored, managed, and, if necessary, mitigated.

LAST BUT NOT LEAST: THE APPENDICES

A business plan shouldn't be a tome. As tempting as it might be to include copious amounts of background material, it is rarely a good idea. The average reader has limited time and patience. Actually, *all* readers have limited time and patience, and it's the rare individual who wants to devote significant amounts of either to poring over the details of someone else's business plan. Keep the body of your plan succinct and targeted and save the elaboration for the appendices. For example, you might want to identify the members of the planning team in an appendix. Other typical appendices include:

- Organizational history
- Any program or partner screens (criteria) created during the process
- A description or visual representation of the organization's current slate of programs
- Market data: additional detail that backs up the presentation in the body of the plan
- The results of any research that was done (e.g., on competitors, partnership models, best practices; stakeholder interviews)
- Organizational charts, if not included in the body of the plan
- Financial projections: the full statements, if not included in the body of the plan, and a review of the different scenarios tested, if helpful; include any additional detail on the assumptions that fed into the projections and scenarios
- **A list and description of founding partners and/or member organizations, if the focus of the plan is a partnership among**

many organizations, as well as any MOU agreed to by the partners.

As we've stated before, every plan is different. Not every situation calls for the same level of detail. Consider the focus of your plan, the complexity of what you are proposing, your audience's information needs, and the nature of any decisions that will be made based on what you present in your business plan. You may find that less is more (always nice), or it may be that, in your situation, more is more. Appendices allow you to keep the body of the plan focused without shortchanging the reader looking for that "more": an additional level of detail that will help someone to better understand your conclusions.

> Keep the body of your plan succinct and targeted and save the elaboration for the appendices.

CASE STUDY: KNOWLEDGE FORCE – PART 9

Sharon, working closely with Amy, Henry, and Deborah and with specific input from the management team, had pulled together the many elements of the business plan into a comprehensive document. Although only 25 pages in length, the appendices added another 40 pages of background information, market research, and financial statements.

Throughout the planning process, those involved had recognized that ongoing evaluation would continue to be critical to Knowledge Force's leadership position in its field. Since the organization's founding, formal internal and external evaluation had been a high priority. It informed curricular and program practices and also provided an edge in fundraising and marketing. In fact, the proven success of Knowledge Force's approach was identified as a distinct competitive advantage that other groups could not claim, and the entire leadership team was committed to maintaining this edge going forward.

The planning team had built a new position, Director of Learning, into its projections, but hiring for that position would not be triggered until revenues grew another $1 million-$1.5 million. In the meantime, the plan suggested clearly designating who would be responsible for cultivating relationships with academic researchers and developing an internal culture that promoted experimentation and sharing of new approaches across sites.

"Although most of the plan is in place," Sharon stated at the start of a planning team draft report review meeting, "we have one more big issue to look at. We need to make recommendations about implementation milestones and create a good 'Plan B' if you're not meeting those markers."

"It's about time we're talking about that!" chimed in Sofia. "I'm willing to go along with the recommendation to expand, but you've heard me say over and over, 'if the assumptions are right.' And I want to know that my company's investment means Knowledge Force is doing better work. How will I know that?" Sofia looked straight at Amy.

Once again, Amy knew that, while Sofia could be irritating, she could also be right. Knowledge Force was committed to regular evaluation of its programs; in fact, it was the field leader in submitting its methodology and results to scrutiny. But Amy also knew that the planning team had not yet built that same plan for scrutiny into the business plan. Even though they had secured the start-up capital they needed, she knew that, if the program were not sustainable over time, she'd find herself shuttering expansion sites once again in three or four years. After spending her first years on the job cleaning up the mistakes made last time, she had no intention of letting this round of growth drag Knowledge Force down again.

"Let's look at our financial projections again," said Sharon, "and identify the critical points for expenditures. It is at those points that you can stop and make sure you're on track with your plans and make adjustments before it's too late."

"Perfect," said Amy. "And then, if I'm not mistaken, we're ready to share this with the full board. Onward!"

BUSINESS PLAN AS ROADMAP

We can't emphasize enough that a good business plan is a roadmap. It is limited by what is known at the time it is written. The world is constantly changing, and not everything will happen quite as you hope or expect. You might have recruited the best leaders since Abraham Lincoln's "team of rivals," but, if one of them decides it's time for a career change, you'll need to adjust.[25] Infrastructure investments that look ideal on paper may not be possible if that initial investment of capital you planned on isn't forthcoming. And the level of demand that months of research has led you to believe is absolutely there (really!) may not materialize if the economy takes a tumble. A business plan is an informed guess—well thought out, built on reasoned assumptions, and supported by solid research but, for all that, still a guess. This is why the credibility and track record of the leadership team are so important: ultimately, that team will make the necessary adjustments and keep the venture on track. A great business plan shows how that team thinks.

25. Succession planning, though outside the scope of this book, is a critical function in any nonprofit. Thinking about the implications of a change in leadership is particularly important when launching a new venture.

CHAPTER 8
BUSINESS PLAN AS DECISION-MAKING TOOL

The primary function of any business plan is to inform decision making and implementation. No matter how well-researched or beautifully presented the final business plan, if it does not facilitate good decisions, it has not helped. Reaching this successful conclusion depends on paving the way right from the outset. In Chapter 1, we described a process for formulating the questions you hope the business planning process will help you to answer, and we recommended defining both the decision makers and the audience for the plan. If the focus of the business plan is a partnership, the decision makers may hail from several organizations, and each may have different information needs and a different decision-making culture or, in the case of public agencies, even a legal mandate for how the decision is made.

As an example, we once worked with a group of organizations that came together to provide social services at a large inner-city school site. The process for making shared decisions involved one representative from each partner serving on a steering committee. The committee was empowered to approve new programs for the school site, manage core staff, and oversee the partnership's budget. A few weeks into the process, however, the public partner informed the others that it could no longer be a part of the steering committee. The public agency's legal counsel had advised that its participation in decision making around staffing for the initiative could create legal liabilities for the county. This initially created great anxiety and not a little turmoil, but eventually the partners reached agreement on how to govern (the public agency representative became a "non-member participant" in the steering committee), and the partnership thrived. Knowing the public agency's situation from the outset, however, might have led to a smoother launch.

Likewise, decisions may not all be made in one place. For example, the board of directors of a nonprofit may be responsible for the decision to budget for and launch a program expansion into a new area. The Executive Director and management staff, however, may be responsible for carrying out the mandate by setting program pricing, securing a marketing consultant to plan promotion of the effort, and deciding how to increase administrative staff to meet growing demand.

Be clear what decisions will need to be made and by whom. Then determine the process each decision maker will use. Often, these issues can be vetted in the planning committee, even if the final decision lies with different leaders or groups. At the beginning of the process, lay all the critical decisions out on a timeline, identifying who is responsible for the final determination, and get everyone to agree on the process to be used.

ENGAGING YOUR KEY COLLEAGUES IN THE DECISION

Some people are risk takers while others are quite conservative.

Some people know their mind as soon as they hear an idea, but others need to mull it over.

Some people need lots of data while others just want to look you in the eye and measure your level of self-confidence.

These and other dynamics of personal preference and decision-making style are probably present in every human organization. One of the easiest ways to derail a decision-making process is to assume that everyone looks at things in the same way: your way. Make time for the mullers to mull; make raw data available to those who want the details; urge patience on the part of quick movers; develop go/no-go points for the cautious. By accommodating all reasonable requests during the decision-making process, you will do more than simply ease that process; you will also improve the final product, while building trust. When a group of people is responsible for making a decision, some shared discomfort usually means the process is just about right: the person who wants reams of detailed information feels there isn't enough, while the person who needs to understand the concept but doesn't want to delve deeply into the details feels that the process is weighed down by a focus on minutiae.

ATTRACTING FUNDERS TO A WINNING IDEA

Many potential funders will initially be attracted to your ideas because they care about your cause. But to move them into the "sold" column, you must meet *their* needs, not yours. A good business plan can go a long way toward assuring funders that the investment they are contemplating will pay off. It can also show them "in black and white" that they are not signing on to an open-ended commitment. Especially for a new venture or a sizable growth strategy, sustainability is a major concern for funders. A convincing demonstration that, over the first few years, a promising new idea can become self-sustaining may be just the assurance that a potential funder needs to move forward with you. We have seen good business plans produce seven-figure funding commitments. Fulfillment of these large commitments is usually tied to meeting specific milestones laid out in the plan: if, at the end of year one, you hit certain milestones, for example, the funder will support year two. Likewise, most funders are supportive of reasonable and necessary changes in the plan as it is implemented, as long as the analysis is strong and the communication direct.

ACKNOWLEDGING WHEN A VENTURE OR AN IDEA IS UNWORKABLE

One of the more painful experiences a nonprofit leader with a big idea can face is the recognition that, despite every good intention and the combined creativity of the organization's leaders, the program, initiative, or even the whole nonprofit enterprise is simply not sustainable. When this happens, there is a temptation to reject one's own business plan, blame skeptical board members, fire the consultants, or reinterpret reality to fit with the future you would prefer.

A common example of this phenomenon is the capital campaign undertaken despite a dismal report from the fundraising consultant's feasibility study. Usually, the campaign quickly stalls, leaving a legacy of unnecessary costs and embarrassment for the organization. Closer to our theme, let's imagine that the business plan for a new facility makes clear that the organization will not be able to operate the considerably larger space sustainably, despite the fact that money is available to build it. The nation is littered with beautiful new buildings that have weakened or even killed their owners with increased and unsustainable operating costs. The lesson is clear: if the project is infeasible or, as in the previous example, there is money to build but not to operate the new facility, it is better to pull back and regroup. A great business plan provides the opportunity to rethink and start over, which is far less painful than launching a failed venture, particularly when that failure could bankrupt the organization.

Fear of the unknown is natural, as is a certain reluctance to take risks. Every business plan, every innovative initiative will involve unknowns, or assumptions that will have to be proven. There is never a 100% guarantee that your initiative will succeed, no matter how positive a picture the business plan paints. Some risk is good and will spur the organization to be attentive, to set meaningful implementation milestones, and to build in a strong evaluation and learning plan throughout the launch period and beyond. It is important to differentiate between this type of risk—which indicates the need for thorough planning and sound execution—and risk stemming from more serious red flags, true indicators that the endeavor is unlikely to be successful.

CONCLUSION
DARE² SUCCEED –
GO OUT AND MAKE IT HAPPEN!

Our world is full of problems waiting to be solved. Over the past half century, nonprofit organizations have become our nation's primary vehicle for social innovation and transformation. Thus, it is no surprise that the need for the work of organizations like yours is only growing. Of course, that work is not getting any easier, and securing adequate funding is, for many nonprofits, harder than ever.

For many years, beginning in the 1960s, nonprofits were buoyed by growth in both public expenditure for social causes and private philanthropy. That growth was driven by a belief that we could, working together, solve our major social problems. The War on Poverty was perhaps the greatest expression of that can-do attitude. For decades pioneering work in many fields was conducted by visionary leaders, communities, and organizations that often paid too little attention to economic and operational considerations. They just went out and did it—often quite successfully but sometimes making quite an organizational mess along the way. More recently, however, the nonprofit sector has entered an era of limited and decreasing public funding, stagnant philanthropy, compassion fatigue, and greater competition from both nonprofit and for-profit actors in virtually every sphere of endeavor. In this more complex and risky operating environment, bold innovators continue to tackle ever more difficult social problems through their communities, organizations, and networks.

While there is no shortage of great ideas, inspiring leaders, and committed activists today, there is in fact a serious shortage of funds—and of public will. We created the business planning methodology described in this book in an attempt to provide some simple guidelines and tools that will help great innovators—like you—to continue to think up bold ideas to then turn them into a sustainable reality. The work of creating a more just and equitable world requires strong organizations that can carry out bold ideas, accelerating social change. A business plan is only one tool for doing so, but it is a powerful tool in the right hands: yours.

APPENDIX A
SAMPLE BUSINESS PLAN: KNOWLEDGE FORCE

Knowledge Force is a fictional organization. The business plan included here is a sample only and reflects the conditions and decisions described in the case study. While appendices are referenced in the body of the plan, they have not been included here.

BUSINESS PLAN:
2013-2015

EXECUTIVE SUMMARY

Knowledge Force believes passionately in a future where every child knows how to read. Its mission—to increase literacy among low-income students in kindergarten through grade three—is a stepping stone to this future. Through its award-winning programs, Knowledge Force trains volunteers—typically, retirees—to be school-based tutors; their efforts currently impact the lives of 15,000 students per year.

Knowledge Force, which has built a national presence by establishing local offices and now has operations in eight metropolitan areas, is poised to grow. The need for what Knowledge Force offers is both tremendous and widespread. Childhood poverty rates are increasing nationwide, and schools are struggling to serve ever-greater numbers of students who enter school without the skills needed to learn how to read. A closer look at rates of both poverty and literacy across the country confirms that numerous metropolitan areas could benefit from the Knowledge Force program, which has been proven effective time and again.

Over the course of many months and after undertaking an in-depth planning process[1], however, Knowledge Force has come to believe that our current growth strategy—continued expansion of the current model to even more metropolitan areas—is not necessarily the best way to maximize impact. Instead, Knowledge Force must emphasize greater depth within individual metropolitan areas, utilizing *more* volunteers to reach *more* students in *more* schools. This is a new approach to expansion (without changes to the essential elements of the program), and over the next three years, Knowledge Force will pilot it through an aggressive expansion into one metropolitan area: Baltimore, MD. Baltimore is an ideal market for Knowledge Force, having both great need among children and high numbers of retirees, the demographic most likely to volunteer as Knowledge Force tutors. As important, other tutoring programs currently operating in and around Baltimore are either not well-known locally or have not been shown to be as effective as Knowledge Force.

1. See Appendix A for an overview of the planning process.

Key Metrics

Knowledge Force will pursue an ambitious growth strategy that will double the number of children it serves—from 15,000 to 30,000 children—in a three-year period. It will do this while reducing its overall cost per child from $200 to $150 and becoming financially self-sufficient by Year 3. The strategy, if successful, will enable Knowledge Force to launch a new phase of growth that will bring the organization and its services to many more children.

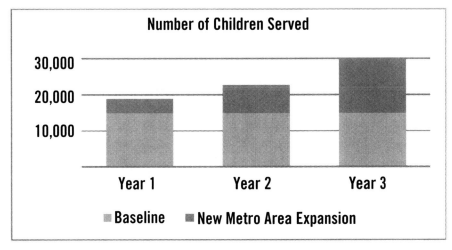

30,000 Children in Three Years: By expanding rapidly to 60 schools in a single metropolitan area, Knowledge Force will grow from 15,000 students served to 30,000 in three years.

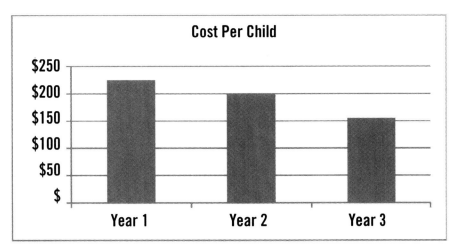

Cost Per Child: Focusing large-scale expansion in a single metropolitan area will allow Knowledge Force to achieve certain economies of scale that will enable it to reduce its cost per child by 25%.

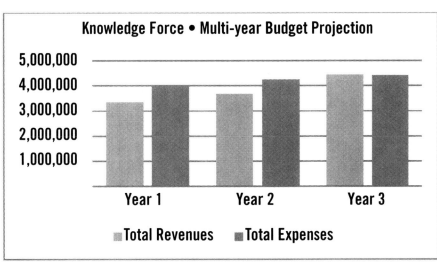

Achieving Financial Sustainability: Assuming it is successful in achieving each of its growth objectives, Knowledge Force will have a sustainable budget of $4.6 million by Year 3, requiring no further growth capital for this particular expansion.

Capital/Start-Up

This scale-up plan will require an initial investment of $1.275 million, of which $300,000 has already been raised. An additional $800,000 has been committed in the form of four challenge grants, one from each of the four major textbook publishers. It is expected that the remaining funds will come primarily from large foundations and other institutional funders.

Ongoing Support

By the third year after the Baltimore launch, the overall Knowledge Force budget is projected to reach $4.6 million annually. Current political and economic trends suggest that federal sources are unlikely to offer significant new support, either now or in the near future. However, Knowledge Force has a demonstrated track record of earning a significant portion of its revenues through payments from schools (in the form of program fees), and this revenue will cover a significant portion of the ongoing Baltimore metropolitan region budget. Knowledge Force succeeds in securing school fees both because its model has been rigorously evaluated and proven effective and also because it is a relatively low-cost means of achieving the schools' own desired ends.

Other potential sources of funding include community foundations, other local funders, and individual donors. Preliminary research into both foundation giving priorities and the funding mechanisms employed by other national education organizations with local branches was encouraging. At scale, the Baltimore area office would need to raise approximately $1 million to support overall operations of the program—a reasonable goal given the prospects already identified.

School Contributions

Knowledge Force currently operates in approximately 60 schools and successfully earns between $5,000 and $25,000 per school. As the organization invests in rapid expansion in the Baltimore metropolitan area, it will pursue a more uniform financing model. Projections assume an average per-school contribution of $15,000, consistent with current experience. Only by engaging schools as contributing partners will the program be sustainable over time.[2]

---

2. While it is true that local school districts are working with increasingly tight budgets, a high percentage of the schools served by Knowledge Force qualify for Title I funds and thus have access to resources to support literacy programs for children in poverty.

VISION, MISSION, AND DESIRED IMPACT

Knowledge Force believes passionately in a future where every child knows how to read, and it seeks to fulfill this dream by increasing literacy among low-income students in kindergarten through grade three. Through its award-winning programs, Knowledge Force trains volunteers—typically, retirees—to be school-based tutors; their efforts currently impact the lives of 15,000 students per year. Expansion into the Baltimore metropolitan area will double that number within three years, bringing the total to 30,000. This expansion is a pilot: the lessons learned will inform hoped-for expansion into other areas in the future. The ultimate goal—to eradicate childhood illiteracy across the country—will be achieved one city, one school, one volunteer, one student at a time.

> By 2015, Knowledge Force will help **30,000** children per year learn to **read**.

ORGANIZATION

Programs

Knowledge Force has built its evidence-based programs over 15 years by focusing on students in kindergarten through third grade (this being the age where interventions aimed at the acquisition of reading skills have the greatest impact), with an emphasis on those at risk for falling behind grade level. The Knowledge Force model is heavily dependent on volunteers, each of whom works in the classroom with small groups of children. It was founded by two talented, retired teachers who realized that their network of colleagues was also retiring from teaching, and—like them—these dedicated professionals were still interested in being engaged with their communities.

Knowledge Force programs have been proven effective time and time again. A 2006 university-sponsored evaluation of the program showed a substantial increase in literacy among Knowledge Force students compared with those in other tutoring programs. Ongoing evaluations have resulted in an evolving approach to both training and tutoring that has consistently proved effective. The benefit extends beyond students: two different studies have shown that retirees participating as volunteers improved their quality of life. Knowledge Force's commitment to improvement and proof of its value through multiple studies has led to receipt of several national and local awards for educational and civic excellence.

Structure and Staffing

Knowledge Force has built a national presence by establishing local offices; it now operates in eight metropolitan areas. Each locality, typically staffed by a Program Manager and a Program Assistant, is responsible for the entire array of programming: cultivating school relationships, recruiting and training volunteers, and reaching out to local funders. The national office, based in Washington, DC, provides the curriculum, supports training and fundraising efforts, manages program evaluation, and provides all administrative support, including payroll, human resources, and information-technology services.

Knowledge Force operates its programs with a combination of paid and volunteer staff, leveraging the use of volunteers in three key capacities: as School Coordinators, Team Leaders, and Classroom Volunteers. School Coordinators supervise Team Leaders, supporting programming at up to four schools. Team Leaders are assigned to one school each, managing and supporting up to 20 Classroom Volunteers.

Although this staffing model has worked well to date, aggressive expansion into the Baltimore metropolitan area will require additional paid staff working at the local level in order to recruit and train the large number of volunteers needed, as well as to cultivate relationships with key stakeholders. This investment will allow Knowledge Force to engage much more deeply in the Baltimore region, both growing and focusing its impact in ways not possible with the current staffing model.

THE MARKET

Market Trends and Market Needs

Research has shown that poverty is the single best predictor of a child's failure to achieve in school,[3] and numerous studies confirm that children from low-income families experience multiple barriers to literacy. Literacy, in turn, is an important predictor of success in school and in life. Unfortunately, data released by the U.S. Census Bureau in September 2011 reveals 46.2 million poor people in America, the largest number in the past 52 years. One in three of America's poor were children—16.4 million—over 950,000 more than in 2010.[4] With poverty rates increasing nationwide, ensuring that every child develops the literacy skills she needs to succeed is only getting more difficult.

---

3. Brizius, J. A., & Foster, S. A. (1993). *Generation to Generation: Realizing the Promise of Family Literacy.* High/Scope Press
4. http://www.childrensdefense.org/newsroom/cdf-in-the-news/press-releases/2011/american-dream-vanishing-for.html

The economic downturn has made literacy work more challenging in other ways as well. Many foundations are making cuts to their education portfolios in favor of protecting the foundation's job-readiness efforts with young adults and the unemployed. Several Knowledge Force competitors have experienced a slowdown in funding for their programs, and many school districts have lost at least some access to quality tutoring programs in recent years.[5]

Although the economy has been improving, economists expect employment to stay low by historical standards and poverty to remain high. The need for Knowledge Force's high-impact, low-cost services will remain significant.

Target Market

Knowledge Force defines its target market as a metropolitan area with high poverty, low literacy rates, and high numbers of retirees. Research conducted in the course of the planning process confirmed that communities with high poverty and low literacy rates also tend to have higher numbers of Title 1 schools[6] and receive significant Supplemental Educational Services (SES) funds[7], money that supports free tutoring or remedial help to students in such subjects as reading, language arts, and math. Since school districts with access to this funding are more likely to be able to pay for Knowledge Force's services (and more likely to need them), the Knowledge Force planning team prioritized possible expansion areas using three factors: poverty rates, literacy rates, and numbers of Title 1 schools.

> Data released by the U.S. Census Bureau in September 2011 reveals 46.2 million poor people in America, the largest number in the last 52 years.

Further consideration was given to the size of each community: the business planning process indicated that a large-scale expansion in a single metropolitan area would require confirmed potential to serve at least 60 Title I and underperforming schools for the effort to become financially sustainable. Because very large markets, such as New York City and Los Angeles, are uniquely competitive, Knowledge Force looked specifically at secondary or mid-level markets for easier entry.

---

5. Interviews conducted over the course of the planning process with foundation program officers and school district officials around the country. See Appendix B for a list of those interviewed.

6. Title I, a provision of the Elementary and Secondary Education Act passed in 1965, is a program created by the United States Department of Education to distribute funding to schools and school districts with a high percentage of students from low-income families. To be an eligible Title I school, at least 40% of a school's students must be from families defined by the United States Census as low-income.

7. Established in 2002 by the federal No Child Left Behind Act, SES was created to improve academic achievement for students whose math and reading scores are among the lowest in the nation's public schools. Baltimore City Public Schools, like other large urban districts, is a prime beneficiary of this federal program. [http://www.abell.org/pubsitems/arn911.pdf]

Table 1 summarizes data for the top ten prospects based on the criteria outlined above. Further evaluation confirmed that all areas being considered had a significant enough number of older adults who could be engaged as volunteers. It is important to note that the numbers shown in the table represent schools located within the named city only and do not include schools and students in districts serving outlying suburban areas. Including those schools could potentially double the number of students served by a particular metro area office. (Detailed data is included in Appendix C.)

	Children in Poverty (percent) 2010[3]	K-3 Title 1 Schools *in named school district only* (approximate)	Percent of 4th-grade public-school students performing below grade level in reading in that state[4]
Detroit, MI	54%	92	70
Cleveland, OH	53%	107	64
Milwaukee, WI	46%	116	67
Miami, FL	45%	92	64
Fresno, CA	43%	80	76
Memphis, TN	40%	102	72
Dallas, TX	38%	174	72
Baltimore, MD	37%	104	63
Philadelphia, PA	36%	211	63
Phoenix, AZ	31%	147	75

Table 1: Top Ten Prospects for Knowledge
Force Expansion

The final, "non-mission" criteria Knowledge Force established for considering expansion sites was the availability of local funding. Current experience is that no metropolitan area is completely supported by earned revenue (school fees); contributed income is essential to sustain the program.

Choosing Baltimore

While there is much to recommend each of the sites highlighted in Table 1, the Baltimore metropolitan area offers a unique opportunity and is thus an ideal choice for expansion at this time. First, the geography of Maryland is such that a concentrated effort based in Baltimore but extending out to

[3] http://datacenter.kidscount.org/data/acrossstates/Rankings.aspx?loct=3&by=v&order=d&ind=43&dtm=322&tf=133
[4] http://www.childrensdefense.org/child-research-data-publications/state-of-americas-children-2011/education.html

nearby communities with need could conceivably impact the entire state in a major way. Second, the area's proximity to Washington, DC—and thus the Knowledge Force national office—will allow greater participation of national staff in the piloting process. Lastly, a current Maryland donor, working in partnership with the Executive Director and a member of the Knowledge Force board, has helped secure commitments for 50% of the growth capital required for expansion into this particular location.

Competitors

Each metropolitan area is unique, and thus the identity, prominence, and efficacy of Knowledge Force's competitors vary depending on location. In general, however, Knowledge Force faces competition from both for-profit and nonprofit providers of tutoring services. As part of the business planning process, Knowledge Force surveyed three prominent national competitors and summarized the key characteristics of each; results are shown in Table 2.

	For-profit ABC	Nonprofit LMN	Nonprofit XYZ
Overview of Programs/ Services	Serves K-12 Serves both low-income students through school contracts and paying students through parent payment	Serves K-8 Program built on paying parents to tutor both their own children and schoolmates	Serves K-5 Hires tutors from all facets of community, usually individuals seeking extra income Approach built around strong methodology similar to KF
Geographic Focus	National chain operated through local franchises	National, with a strong presence in major cities and the East	Nationally, with greatest presence in the Southwest
Client/Constituent Focus	Recent graduates Public brand/ communication aimed at both the upper middle class (parents able to pay) and school districts	Parents	Schools and administrators
Primary Funding Sources	100% fee-driven, paid by both schools and individual families	Individual and local contributions School contracts	School contracts
Key Strengths and Points of Differentiation	High cachet by hiring only young adults with advanced degrees to provide tutoring services	Grassroots base among parents and community leaders Local knowledge related to parent base No consistent methodology beyond parent involvement Results not independently evaluated	Strong presence among educators; close relationships with school administrators; strong marketing presence in education conferences and journals
Service Gap (needs the organization is not meeting)	Limited ability to contract with schools because of high-cost model	No consistent methodology beyond parent involvement Results not independently evaluated	Unknown

Table 2: Competitor Analysis, Primary National Competitors

A similar analysis of tutoring programs in the state of Maryland was conducted. This summary can be found in Appendix D.

Positioning Statement

Building from its understanding of its competitors, Knowledge Force has identified its own competitive advantages.

Superior Outcomes. Formal, independent evaluation has demonstrated repeatedly that the Knowledge Force methodology is effective at increasing literacy, both in absolute terms and compared with other tutoring approaches.

Volunteer Model. Knowledge Force has demonstrated a unique ability to successfully recruit, train, and manage an extensive volunteer corps, primarily of retirees.

Cost. Because of the extensive use of volunteers and the group-tutoring methodology, the superior outcomes are delivered at a very low per-student cost.

Based on this understanding, Knowledge Force has articulated its positioning statement, or description of benefit.

For school districts, Knowledge Force brings a proven methodology, a track record of success, and an inexpensive means to increase literacy among K-3 students. While many tutoring programs struggle to demonstrate results, Knowledge Force emphasizes ongoing evaluation, continuous improvement, and proof of impact. The result: independent evaluations have shown a substantial increase in literacy among Knowledge Force students compared with those in other tutoring programs and that the cost-per-student for achieving this success is significantly lower than the alternatives.

For potential volunteers, Knowledge Force offers an opportunity to engage in the community in a meaningful way, supported by a comprehensive training and development program. Independent evaluations have shown Knowledge Force volunteers to have a higher quality of life as a result of their work with the students.

MANAGEMENT AND OPERATIONS

Governance

The Knowledge Force Board of Directors is made up of 14 individuals from the public, private, and nonprofit sectors. It has played an active oversight role since the organization's founding (though only recently began focusing on resource development) and will continue to play an important role throughout the expansion period. Board members have committed to playing an active role in both fundraising and "friend raising," cultivating relationships in their personal and professional networks and forging new ties in the communities where Knowledge Force has—or will have—a presence. As the organization's governing body, the board will actively follow the expansion effort and work with the Executive Director to monitor progress against the plan.

Board President Maria Fernandez is a retired Superintendent of Schools from Phoenix, AZ. She previously served as Superintendent in Riverside, CA, and Albuquerque, NM. Although she began her career as a teacher, she became particularly interested in learning methodologies and spent five years pursuing her Ph.D. in Education and five more as an Associate Professor of Education at the University of Arizona in Tucson, specializing in childhood learning and program evaluation.

There is currently one opening on the board; the Governance (Nominating) Committee is working to identify a high-profile Maryland candidate with connections in the education sector and experience in organizational growth.

A full list of board members is included in Appendix E.

Management

The Knowledge Force Team is led by CEO Amy Rivera. Amy has worked in education her entire professional career: she spent 13 years teaching elementary school in Tucson before being hired as Executive Director of Southwestern Tutorial. While leading Southwestern, she doubled the budget and expanded the organization to new areas of Arizona and into Nevada. She was hired as the Knowledge Force Executive Director three years ago and, in that time, has increased the budget by 25%, moved operations into a surplus, and added new academic partners for program evaluation. Amy received both her B.A. and Master's in Education at University of Arizona at Tucson.

Chief Program Officer Henry Jiang received his Ph.D. at Stanford University School of Education and stayed on as an Assistant Professor for four years. Seeking more hands-on work with at-risk students, he became an elementary school teacher in the Ravenswood School District in East Palo Alto, CA, while maintaining part-time status at Stanford. He came to Knowledge Force eight years ago and has served as the Program Director ever since, leveraging his academic relationships to bring rigorous independent evaluation to the Knowledge Force methodology.

CFO Deborah Robinson received both her undergraduate degree in Business Administration and her Master's in Financial Analysis from the University of San Francisco. After working for several small businesses in the San Francisco area, she sought out more meaningful work in the nonprofit sector. She joined Knowledge Force 10 years ago as a Program Assistant in the Oakland Metro office. Her aptitude for business and her financial skills were quickly noted, and Knowledge Force supported her to return to USF to pursue her Master's in Financial Analysis, which she was awarded six years ago. Following graduation, she was promoted to Administrative Coordinator in the national office and then to CFO three years later.

Development Director Olivia Ryan has been with Knowledge Force for just over one year. With 11 years' experience leading development efforts at nonprofits with budgets between $5 million and $15 million, Olivia has brought considerable energy and insight to the development function at Knowledge Force. In one year, she has both expanded the organization's national fundraising capacity and put in place an aggressive program of individual and major donor solicitation that is poised to ramp up dramatically.

Organizational Structure and Staffing

The Knowledge Force organizational structure is heavily—almost exclusively—weighted to program work with nearly all staff reporting up to the Chief Program Officer. The organization recently expanded its centralized capacity marginally by upgrading the national development capacity and adding new administrative support.

Effective management of program staff dispersed throughout the country, and effective relationship building with local school districts, requires on-the-ground leadership. Therefore, most program management lies with two Senior Managers overseeing the Eastern and Western regions of the country. With routine management resting with the Senior Managers, Henry, the Chief Program Officer, is able to focus on program evaluation, curriculum development, and general systemic improvements.

Knowledge Force is a volunteer-driven organization. At the local level, Program Managers are responsible for overseeing all local volunteer activity. They do this with the support of several senior-level volunteer positions: (Volunteer) School Coordinators, and (Volunteer) Team Leaders.

Each School Coordinator manages the volunteer function at four schools, working closely with the Program Manager and Program Assistant. School Coordinators supervise three to five Team Leaders, each of whom works at one school and supervises approximately 20 volunteers. Team Leaders work in partnership with other Team Leaders, their School Coordinator, and the Program Manager to ensure consistent services across schools.

Following is both a current organizational chart (Figure 1) and a chart specific to the Baltimore area expansion (Figure 2). New (proposed) positions are shown with a dotted outline.

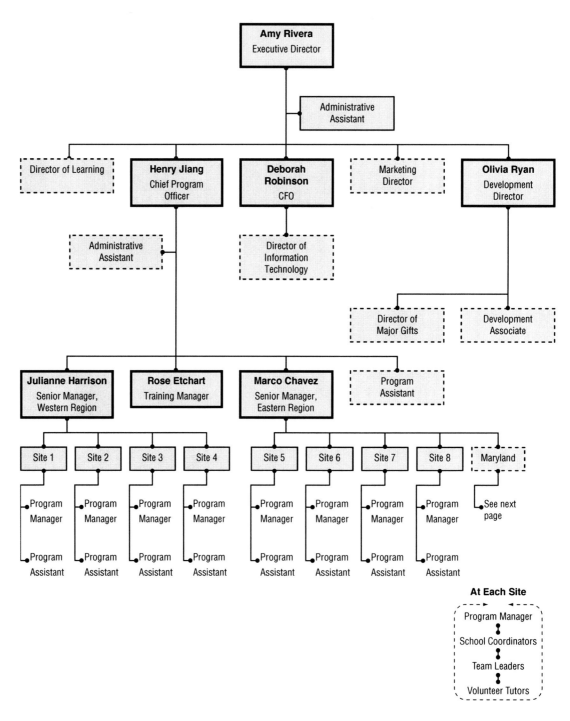

Figure 1: Knowledge Force Organizational Chart

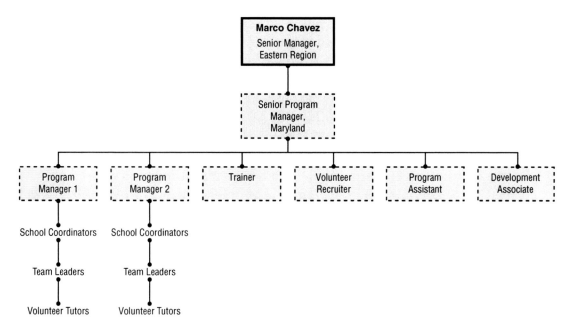

Figure 2: Knowledge Force Organizational Chart (continued)

Operations and Infrastructure

Expansion into Baltimore will require changes to the current Knowledge Force operating model, both locally and in national operations.

Local

At full roll-out, the Baltimore office will be the nexus for fully half of Knowledge Force's programmatic activity. The staffing required to ramp up to and maintain this level of service must be more robust than in other metropolitan areas.

- Rather than being led by a Program Manager, the office will be led by a Senior Program Manager. This position will be unique to the Maryland expansion. Based in Baltimore, this individual will be responsible for establishing Knowledge Force in Baltimore City public schools and then expanding to other high-poverty areas throughout the state.

- Two Program Managers, a Volunteer Recruiter, and a Trainer will report directly to the Senior Program Manager. The Trainer will maintain a "dotted-line" relationship to the national Training Manager.

- Additional local fundraising capacity will be provided by a Development Associate, who will report to the Senior Program Manager but have a "dotted-line" relationship to the national Development Department.

National

Additional capacity will be needed at the national office to support both program and operations.

- A new Director of Learning will ensure that training and tutoring methodologies are consistent (and of consistently high quality) throughout the country. She or he will also be responsible for maintaining a robust program evaluation process, including both internal tracking and independent program review—and for translating what is learned into new or modified curriculum. Since independent evaluation is carried out through pro bono university projects, the Director of Learning must maintain strong relationships with university education departments and researchers.

- The dramatic ramp-up in school contracts will require greater relationship building capacity, which will be guided and supported by a new Marketing Director. The person filling this position should have high visibility and be able to open doors for the Senior Program Manager (in Baltimore), Program Managers, and other staff. The position will be focused initially in Maryland but will be expected to create a "strike team" to develop relationships in other communities in advance of future expansion.

- Training a large number of volunteers in a specific methodology will require sophisticated training skills. The current Training Manager position will be augmented with local staff in Baltimore, but demands on national staff will be monitored, and a staff expansion may be necessary.

- Internal systems for accounting, contract management, and information technology will need upgrades. In the short term, these responsibilities will be handled by the CFO; outside assistance (e.g., from technology consultants) will be sought as necessary. Longer term, a new Director of Information Technology will be brought in to oversee information-technology strategy and services.

- As demonstrated in this business plan, the Knowledge Force model can be largely self-sustaining once a program is established in a metropolitan area. However, start-up funds are necessary. The national office must expand its fundraising capacity to bring in "investment" dollars to move into and stabilize new (or expanded) metropolitan areas. Two new development positions—Director of Major Gifts and Development Associate—will be needed.

Growing rapidly and successfully will require careful attention to the timing of key hires. Table 3 summarizes the timeline upon which the Knowledge Force multi-year budget was based.

Incremental FTE Required: Baltimore Metropolitan Area			
	Year 1	Year 2	Year 3
Senior Program Manager	1.00		
Program Manager 1	1.00		
Program Manager 2		1.00	
Volunteer Recruiter	1.00		
Trainer	1.00		
Development Associate	1.00		
Program Assistant	1.00		

Incremental FTE Required: Knowledge Force National Office			
	Year 1	Year 2	Year 3
Development Associate		1.00	
Director of Major Gifts			1.00
Director of Information Technology			1.00
Administrative Assistant 2		1.00	
Program Assistant			1.00
Director of Learning			1.00
Marketing Director		1.00	

Table 3: Timeline for New Hires

A more detailed timeline incorporating other (non-personnel) implementation milestones is included in Appendix F.

MARKETING AND OUTREACH

Education in the United States is an intensely local business. In order to work successfully with individual school systems, an organization must have the capacity to develop relationships with local leaders and to be responsive to local needs.

Knowledge Force has addressed this need by maintaining local metropolitan offices in the areas it serves. A critical component of each Program Manager's job is to build and maintain a positive relationship with local school leaders. In evaluating its competitors, Knowledge Force recognized that other organizations were more effective at building interest or excitement about their work, even though Knowledge Force had been proven to operate a more effective program. Other organizations have deployed "stars" in education to promote their work, to represent their organization at conferences, and to initiate contacts with local school leaders. Although Knowledge Force has some of this capacity—mostly through board members—it has not been nearly as focused nor as successful in this regard.

Such skills are especially important for an organization in growth mode. Knowledge Force will have to meet, cultivate, and negotiate with a greater number of school leaders in a shorter period of time in order to ramp up aggressively.

With this in mind, Knowledge Force is committed to investing in a Marketing Director. This individual should be well-known in the field, e.g. a former state schools or big-city superintendent, a well-known education researcher, or even a politician known for promoting education. This individual will be responsible for "opening the door" with school leaders and raising the profile of Knowledge Force both nationally and locally.

FINANCIAL PROJECTIONS AND FUND DEVELOPMENT

KEY ASSUMPTIONS

School Revenues

- Each school will pay, on average, $15,000 per year for tutoring services

Capital Requirements

- Start-up will require $1.275 million in growth capital over two years, to support Baltimore area expansion and incremental expansion costs for the national office

- Knowledge Force will be financially self-sufficient by Year 3; no further growth capital will be required for this phase of expansion

- Growth capital will be provided by institutional funders

Financial Sustainability

- At scale (60 schools) the Baltimore area office will generate $900,000 per year in school revenues, covering 92% of its budget

- Supplemental funding will be provided by local foundations and individuals

This business plan details Knowledge Force's proof-of-concept goal to expand from 15,000 students to 30,000 in three years through a rapid expansion in a single new metropolitan area. The proposed expansion will test the organization's ability to scale quickly while demonstrating greatly increased program impact. If successful, Knowledge Force will use what it has learned through this pilot expansion to launch further growth efforts in many more metropolitan areas.

The scale-up plan will require $1.275 million in philanthropic capital to cover deficits en route to a sustainable operation.[8] This includes simultaneous investment in a national infrastructure to support launch in the Baltimore area. It also requires that each participating school pay an average of $15,000 for its services, consistent with fees earned in existing communities.

New Expansion: Baltimore, MD, Metropolitan Area

During the first year of the expansion (which follows a six-month planning phase), Knowledge Force will hire a core team of four local staff members. The next two years will see an aggressive scale-up to 60 schools, reaching 15,000 students and recruiting 1,260 volunteers. At scale, the Baltimore area office will maintain a $1 million budget with seven full-time equivalents (FTEs) and ongoing support from the Knowledge Force national office.

Figure 3 presents the key metrics and multi-year budget numbers for the Baltimore area office. Detailed financial projections for the Baltimore area, along with further explanation of financial drivers and related assumptions, are included in Appendix G.

---

8. See detailed financial projections in Appendix H.

PROGRAM STATISTICS	Year 1	Year 2	Year 3
New Schools	15	30	60
Volunteers	315	630	1,260
Children Served	3,750	7,500	15,000

INCOME STATEMENTS	Year 1	Year 2	Year 3
Revenues			
School Revenues	$ 225,000	$ 450,000	$ 900,000
Foundation Support	16,170	18,582	49,106
Individual Support	40,425	46,456	49,106
Total Revenues	281,595	515,038	998,212
Expenses			
Salary and Benefits	393,750	467,656	479,348
Non-Personnel Costs	414,749	461,463	502,770
Total Expenses	808,499	929,119	982,117
Operating Surplus/Deficit	$ (526,889)	$ (414,051)	$ 16,154

Figure 3: Key Metrics and Multi-year Budget
for Baltimore Area Office

National Infrastructure

To successfully launch operations in the Baltimore area will require substantial investment in a national infrastructure. The national staffing model, shown in Appendix H, reflects both an ongoing commitment to serve existing programs and investment in the additional staffing and infrastructure required to support growth in the Baltimore area—while also ensuring ongoing monitoring to protect the consistent and high-quality services offered nationwide. Additional investment will be allocated to consulting services to support the growth and organizational change process.

Figure 4 presents projected incremental costs within the national office budget.

PROJECTIONS	Year 1	Year 2	Year 3
Personnel	$325,000	$384,375	$446,516
Professional Fees	75,000	75,000	75,000
Travel & Other	10,250	11,225	12,250
Total	$410,250	$470,600	$533,766

Figure 4: Incremental Costs to National Budget Attributable to Baltimore Expansion

Overall Budget

KEY ASSUMPTIONS DRIVING BUDGET PROJECTIONS

- Total Students Per School: 250 (average)

- Students Served: 100% of K-3 students in each school will receive a direct benefit/measurable impact

- Growth Trajectory: 15 new schools in Year 1, 30 (total) in Year 2, and 60 (total) in Year 3

- Volunteers: 21 volunteers per school (average)

- (Volunteer) Team Leaders: One leader per school

- (Volunteer) School Coordinators: One coordinator for every four schools

- Stipends: Each School Coordinator and Team Leader receives $1,000 annually

The overall budget projects growth from $3 million (current) to $4.6 million (Year 3). A *pro forma* budget, including detailed revenue projections, is included as Appendix I.

A summary of projected revenues and expenses is shown in Figure 5.

	Year 1 Projection	Year 2 Projection	Year 3 Projection
Operating Revenues			
National Office and Current Program Revenue	$2,987,883	$3,062,580	$3,139,145
New Fundraising by National Office	75,000	100,000	300,000
One-Time Growth Capital (Uncommitted)[9]	425,000	550,000	
One-Time Growth Capital (Committed)[10]	250,000	50,000	—
New Metro Area Expansion	281,595	515,038	998,212
Total Revenues	4,019,478	4,277,618	4,437,356
Operating Expenses			
National Office	1,002,241	1,027,297	1,052,979
National Incremental Expansion Costs	410,250	470,600	533,766
Current Metro Area Programs	1,985,642	2,035,283	2,086,165
New Metro Area Expansion	808,499	929,119	982,117
Total Expenses	4,206,632	4,462,299	4,655,027
Operating Surplus/Deficit	(187,154)	(184,681)	(217,671)
Costs Allocable to New Metro Area	211,874	224,685	238,012
Operating Surplus/Deficit Post Allocation	$ 24,720	$ 40,004	$ 20,341

Figure 5: Knowledge Force Projected Revenues and Expenses, Years 1-3

Revenue Requirements

Significant institutional investment—$1.275 million—will be required to support this effort in the first two years, at which point the operation will become self-sustaining (albeit with ongoing fundraising needs).

Participation by these initial investors in the "proof-of-concept" phase will enable Knowledge Force to demonstrate the viability of the new model and potentially attract new funding for additional growth. To date, Knowledge Force has secured $300,000 in start-up growth capital.

Ongoing Support
As is the case at current program sites, fee-based support from the schools will be the primary source of ongoing revenues for the Baltimore area office, accounting for approximately 92% of revenues by Year 3. The remaining amount will be leveraged from other local sources, including individuals and foundations. The national office will continue to be sustained largely by con-

---

[9] These funds do not include a pledge from several major textbook publishers.
[10] Board-designated commitment of a one-time bequest to be received over two years

tributions from national education funders as well as through some allocation of locally earned revenue for direct program support. The Knowledge Force board has also adopted a plan for increasing its focus on development in an effort to raise new growth capital for future expansion.

EVALUATION AND MEASUREMENT OF IMPACT

Successful implementation of this plan will require careful attention on the part of management as well as regular oversight by the board. If successful, Knowledge Force will—by the end of Year 3—be providing high-quality tutoring services to 30,000 children in a financially sustainable way and, in the process, enriching the lives of several thousand volunteer tutors.

To ensure that this happens, Knowledge Force will articulate and follow a detailed implementation plan that builds in regular checkpoints for both management and board. Executive Director Amy Rivera will have ultimate responsibility for implementation; she will work closely with both her senior management team and (when hired) the Senior Program Manager for Maryland. Status updates will be shared internally on a monthly basis and externally (with key investors) each quarter. Knowledge Force will continue to seek opportunities for programmatic evaluation through current and future relationships with universities and will (as always) share the results with the field while simultaneously using them to improve program and program delivery. Other evaluation resources may be tapped (e.g., professional evaluation firms) if funding becomes available.

Knowledge Force expects that future evaluations will be more comprehensive than in the past, addressing not only program performance but also factors specific to the expansion and the effect of rapid organizational growth. Input will be sought from staff, volunteers, school-district contacts, school principals, teachers, community leaders, key investors, and the children/families served.

RISKS AND RISK MITIGATION

Knowledge Force believes that the research and analysis undertaken in the course of preparing this plan will provide the foundation for a successful model, both in the pilot phase and as the program grows to an even larger scale. However, no plan is without risk. By identifying the following risks, Knowledge Force demonstrates a commitment to monitor its expansion closely, to compare plans with results, and to make corrections throughout implementation.

	Risks	Mitigations
Reputational	Expected funding may not materialize, resulting in start/stop expansion or the need to retrench before a given expansion takes hold Knowledge Force may not dedicate the resources necessary to maintain consistently high quality control throughout all sites and schools	Establish a minimum level of firm cash commitments before moving forward with expansion into any individual location Incorporate new capacity for evaluation and quality control into the expansion plan
Financial	New staff may not be able to secure school contracts quickly, resulting in high investment with low/no financial return	Put responsibility for "informational interviews" with local school districts at national office; hold on hiring staff until a minimum number of districts has expressed interest Ensure that Baltimore area employees have deep relationships in the community
Legal	Working with children brings inherent legal liabilities	Provide training and oversight in strict adherence to national Knowledge Force standards; invest in additional training capacity at the national level to ensure consistent volunteer interactions Include a clause in every contract specifying the roles of both Knowledge Force and the school district in carrying out standards; include verbal discussion of legal risks and responsibilities in a semi-annual district check-in by national staff
Program Integrity	Critical current staff may leave mid-expansion, leaving the organization with insufficient skill sets or human capacity to complete the expansion appropriately Work product of new staff may not initially meet national standards Lack of diversity among retirees may not reflect diversity of students	Create "golden handcuffs" agreement with key managers during implementation period to ensure expert oversight of new metro area Pace implementation of new programs at a level that affords close national and regional oversight, particularly in the first two years Determine whether the diversity of volunteers is a priority and develop strategies to maintain the composition desired

APPENDIX B
FINANCIAL MODEL
TEMPLATE

While you may wish to create a financial model for your proposed program, partnership, venture or growth strategy from scratch, it can often be easier to start with a template. We have created such a tool and made it available on www.turnerpublishing.com/nonprofit-business-plan-financial-model-template.xlsx.

WORKSHEET 1
FORMING YOUR PLANNING TEAM

In a business planning process, the planning team typically includes the CEO and top financial manager (CFO or COO). It may also include other senior staff or program staff with specialized knowledge of the proposed activity; board members; middle managers; and/or front-line staff. In a partnership situation, it would typically include representatives from each potential partner or group of partners.

Begin by identifying any specific skills, knowledge, experience, or connections you will need, then think about what mix of individuals will best provide those while also working well as a team.

Skills, knowledge, experience or connections desired:

- Financial analysis skills
- Knowledge of organizational structures and systems
- Program knowledge
- Experience with starting / growing organizations

- Strong connections with (select): funders, constituents, partners, potential partners,

  _____
- Other: _____
- Other: _____
- Other: _____

NAME	TITLE /POSITION	SPECIFIC SKILLS, KNOWLEDGE, EXPERTISE AND/OR CONNECTIONS
1.		
2.		
3.		
4.		
5.		
6.		
7.		
8.		
9.		
10.		

INDEX

CPSIA information can be obtained at www.ICGtesting.com
Printed in the USA
BVOW050333290113

311844BV00012B/277/P